DATE DUE

~~DE 10 02~~		
MY 2 8 08		
DE 1 9 08		

DEMCO 38-296

Community
Service
and Social Responsibility
in Youth

Community
Service
and Social
Responsibility
in Youth

JAMES YOUNISS & MIRANDA YATES

The University of Chicago Press • Chicago & London

or of the Life Cycle Institute at
 ıs books are *Parents and Peers in Social
Relations and *Adolescents, Parents, and Friends,* both published by the
University of Chicago Press.

Miranda Yates is a postdoctoral fellow at the Center for the Study of Race
and Ethnicity in America and the Center for the Study of Human
Development at Brown University. She was awarded the 1996 Hershel
Thornberg Dissertation Award from the Society for Research on
Adolescence.

The University of Chicago Press, Chicago 60637
The University of Chicago Press, Ltd., London
© 1997 by The University of Chicago
All rights reserved. Published 1997
Printed in the United States of America
06 05 04 03 02 01 00 99 98 97 1 2 3 4 5
ISBN: 0-226-96482-5 (cloth)
ISBN: 0-226-96483-3 (paper)

Library of Congress Cataloging-in-Publication Data

Youniss, James.
    Community service and social responsibility in youth / James
  Youniss and Miranda Yates.
        p.   cm.
    Includes bibliographical references and index.
    ISBN 0-226-96482-5 (cloth). — ISBN 0-226-96483-3 (pbk.)
    1. Young volunteers in social service—Washington, D.C.   2. Afro-
  American youth—Washington, D.C.   3. Identity (Psychology) in
  youth.   I. Yates, Miranda.   II. Title.
  HV40.8.U6Y68   1997
  361.3′7′08309753—dc21   96-53450
                                                                  CIP

∞ The paper used in this publication meets the minimum requirements of
the American National Standard for Information Sciences—Permanence of
Paper for Printed Library Materials, ANSI Z39.48-1984.

This book is dedicated to Robert J. Hoderny (1947–1996).
A friend, teacher, and absolute optimist. Too soon.

CONTENTS

PREFACE

The chief purpose of this book is to present a theoretical rationale for youth's involvement in community service. Our thesis is that youth's participation in solving social problems has the potential to promote the development of personal and collective identity. In our view, identity development requires stepping into history by adopting a respected ideology that connects youth to other generations, gives meaning to present experience, and provides hope for the future. This definition implies agency—a sense that one can make a difference in society—and social responsibility, or concern for society's well-being.

Our theoretical approach was stimulated by having read occasional essays about service experiences from several groups of high school students. One group, a class of juniors in a school in Washington, DC, had produced an especially impressive set of reflections. We discovered that the students were attending a Catholic high school and were primarily Black. To us, the essays seemed important for revealing the developmental possibilities of service and for showing a positive side of Black urban youth that was different from their usual depiction in the media.

We wanted to study a group of adolescents closely in order to understand more about the process that mediates effects of service. So we approached this school, which seemed to have considerable potential for our purposes. We quickly came to a mutual agreement about doing an intensive study of the next year's (1993–94) junior class. We agreed to observe these students as they progressed through a required course on social justice in which service at a soup kitchen was a mandatory and essential part. The present book reports the results of this study and describes our theory on how service stimulates political-moral agency and responsibility.

Because the high school is Catholic and the students are predominately Black, questions might arise about the generality of our theory and findings. First, we note that this is not a statistical study with quantitative measures, a sampling procedure, or a multigroup comparative design. It is rather a study designed to generate qualitative data that reflect students' understandings of service, self, and society. Findings illustrate the theory by helping to articulate its core ideas. If results are found useful, they can be pursued subsequently in more detailed work with more standard methods.

Regarding the school, we recognize that students' service and the program in which it is embedded cannot be separated. The program is grounded in a rich tradition of social justice (Tropman 1995) that gives students a respected ideology to consider and to adopt or reject. As will be argued, youth need to be given clear ideological options so that they can assess possible orientations to society. We are not proposing that the particular ideology of this program be a model for all schools, but we believe that the results show how important an ideological grounding is, especially one that is historically viable and inclusive.

Further regarding the school, we agree with Bryk, Lee, and Holland (1993) that it is useful to describe educational processes that seem to account for effective education. If these processes can be made clear, then they should be potentially transferable to other schools, which may adapt them for their own service programs. This transfer works as readily from private to public schools as from public to private, when educational and developmental processes are the focus.

The students we studied were mainly Black and mainly, but not entirely, middle-class youth from Washington, DC. From our perspective, the task of constructing a viable identity is as important to this specific group of students as to any other adolescents. Therefore, what we learned about identity development from these students ought to be applicable to youth in general.

At the same time, the findings from our sample speak to the literature on the psychological development and education of Black youth. The findings reveal the richness of talent that Black youth possess, and show how one service program gainfully tapped this talent. Thus, not only do the results counter the bleak portraits of Black urban youth in the popular media, but they give educators leads on ways to afford students educational challenges and developmental opportunities.

Our general outlook is that most contemporary youth are positively oriented to their parents, other adults, and normative society. Unfortunately, society is so structured that youth are not needed, and often are not welcomed, in the economic, civil, and cultural tasks of continually renewing society. Part of the recent interest in service is based on the desire to alter this matter and to give youth firsthand experience and socialization as the next generation of democratic citizens. We believe our results provide one example of how this can be effectively accomplished and illustrate why interest in youth service is warranted and worthy of our best educational policy efforts.

This book and the research project it reports required the cooperation and effort of several persons and institutions. The project was run from the Life Cycle Institute at the Catholic University of America, where numerous people contributed in various capacities. They are, alphabetically, Jon Anderson, Marcia Annis, Gerald Condon, Philip Davidson, William Dinges, Mary Anne Ely, Michael Foley, Hans Furth, Tanya Giorgini, Dorothy Kane, Anne Kasprzyk, Michelle Khajavi, John McCarthy, Sheila McGannon, Woinishet Negash, Amy Noll, Mary Jo Pugh, and Linda Sperry.

Several colleagues from other universities were helpful in giving us advice, information, and support. We especially thank William Damon, Connie Flanagan, and Daniel Hart, not just for assistance on this project, but for years of wise counsel and the continued generous sharing of their knowledge of children's and youth's development. We also thank Reed Larson for insightful comments on the manuscript.

Key parts of this project were conceived while one of the authors was in Germany on an award from the Humboldt Foundation, which we thank, along with Manfred Hofer, Lothar Krappmann, Peter Noack, and Hans Oswald. We also thank colleagues at the Max Planck Institute in Berlin, Gus Blasi, Wolfgang Edelstein, and Monika Keller. Meanwhile the other author was at Brown University, where Fayneese Miller and Robert Biral and other members of the Center for the Study of Race and Ethnicity in America, particularly Mika Keezing, Florence Lopes, and JoLee Webb, offered advice and support. She is also grateful to Lynn Davey and Otto Hentz.

We could not have completed the study without the generous financial and intellectual support of the William T. Grant Foundation and its officers, Beatrix Hamburg and Lonnie Sherrod. We acknowledge their support with gratitude.

Robert Hoderny was the essential ingredient who gave this project its heart and direction, enabling it to proceed from a hopeful start to this satisfying conclusion.

David Brent of the University of Chicago Press was, as in the past, a skillful, honest, and professional editor. We thank Joann Hoy for excellent copyediting.

Our spouses, Dorothy and Patrick, were patient as they lent enthusiasm and advice, even as attention was directed away from them to this project for long periods of time. We also thank other family members, especially Peter, Virginia, and Toby Yates.

Last, we thank the students, teachers, and administrators of the fictitiously labeled St. Francis High School and the staff at the soup kitchen for allowing us to study their service program and use their ideas to understand contemporary youth and what community service can contribute to adolescents' identity development. We are particularly indebted to the St. Francis students who taught us how much talent and compassion they, and all youth, have and how ready they are to expend these strengths constructively when adults afford worthwhile opportunities.

CHAPTER ONE

Service for Today's Youth and for the Right Reasons

This book has two primary goals. One is to offer a theoretical framework for understanding how community service can stimulate political-moral development in adolescents. The other is to illustrate this framework with findings from a year-long study of community service by a high school class of predominately Black, middle-class youth. We intend to show how service contributed positively to and was integrated in their ongoing identity development. At present, there are many proposals for mandating service for today's youth. But they are backed by only a weak rationale for why positive benefits should result. We offer a theoretical perspective that spells out the process by which service can make an impact and can serve as a model in the design of service programs and educational policy.

We undertook this study for two reasons. First, the fields of political and moral development appeared to us in need of new kinds of data. In the former area, studies seem stuck on documenting knowledge of formal political systems, to the neglect of investigating ways in which adolescents come to understand how politics works and how they, as individuals, come to define themselves as political agents. This distinction is stated concisely by Richard Flacks's differentiation (1988) between generations that "live history" and generations that "make history." Making history involves working toward goals, working for principles, or trying to alter the course of current events. Living history implies merely accepting present conditions by using them to achieve self-satisfying goals. We viewed community service as giving youth an opportunity to see themselves as political agents in the making of history instead of defining themselves as decent but compliant citizens.

The field of moral development has a parallel problem. For several years, theorists have focused on the criteria for mature moral judgment to the exclusion of interest in the conditions that promote mature moral identity (Blasi 1995). In our view, moral maturity involves the willingness to grasp the moral aspect in everyday events and

1

take action on its behalf. Community service appeared to be an obvious occasion for youth to experience themselves as moral agents, because it promotes action-based engagement with conditions of personal need and social inequality.

Second, during the past decade, community service has been offered as a panacea for an ailing educational system and laxity in American youth. Former Republican president Bush and current Democratic president Clinton promoted legislation that encourages youth to serve in the improvement of their local communities. In our view, the rationale for this movement is thinly based on slogans about combating ascendent individualism and repairing alienation between the generations. The majority of arguments seem to be solipsistic in asserting that service ought to benefit participating youth because service is, in itself, altruistic. A key to this theoretical vagueness is the repeated citation of William James's 1909 essay (1971) on the "moral equivalent of war." Despite James's analytical brilliance, one imagines that, in 85 years, social scientists would have produced enough empirical evidence to support claims that youth's service should produce "healthier fathers" and "better citizens." But claims made today are no more grounded in empirical research and are every bit as idealistic as James's were nearly a century ago.

In following up on this problem, we discovered that there were indeed some data that could be brought to bear on the question of whether service actually benefited participants. Researchers have reported differences between youth with and without service experiences, but left open the question of how service specifically produced positive change (Yates and Youniss 1996b). As developmental psychologists, we accepted this question as a challenge to understand the means by which service makes a positive impact on participating youth. What is it precisely that changes in the participants that allows them to understand other persons, themselves, or society in a new light? If an answer were available, we would know the kinds of effects to anticipate and the developmental processes that mediate them.

In asking the question in this way, we are proposing that the field of community service lacks and needs a theory that clearly justifies demands on youthful energy, modification of school curricula, and expenditures of public and private funds. To this end, in chapter 2 we outline a theoretical conception of service that intertwines with the developmental process of identity construction. This sketch is consciously built on selected portions of Erik Erikson's writings that address the relationship between individual and societal identity. Rather than focusing on the inward search for authenticity and self-validation, we emphasize adolescents' investment in social, political, and moral ideologies. Adolescents cannot survive as free-standing entities, but need to identify with transcendent ideas that provide the self with enduring sources of meaning.

We propose, therefore, that community service offers opportunities for this crucial self-society linkage in identity construction. In working to help other persons in need, adolescents can begin to experience their own agency. They can also begin to ask why people in our society live in such different conditions and do not possess similar basic resources. They may also begin to ask about the political bases of variations in conditions and to question the moral positions that would support either the status quo or reasons for changing it. Most importantly, adolescents who start reflecting in this manner would necessarily consider how they as individuals want to take stands on existing ideologies and so decide whether they might simply live through the present moment of history or take responsibility in the actual remaking of history.

We do not mean to imply that adolescents' decisions are final and determinant of their adult futures. Constructing identity is a lifelong developmental process. But adolescence is the usual time when conscious reflection starts in earnest and the person's future is being designed (Inhelder and Piaget 1958). We recognize that the data to be reported come from novices in the process, and, hence, the concepts they construct do not cast their personalities in permanent form. Nevertheless, the data provide instructive evidence on how service stimulates the identity process during that important time in development when adolescents are open to explore how best to identify themselves with social, political, and moral positions that give their developing identities direction and meaning.

How Should Contemporary Youth Be Characterized?

Community service is frequently recommended as an antidote for ills in society, weaknesses in youth, or both (Dougherty 1993; Conrad and Hedin 1991). We will now offer a brief discussion of these views in order to propose a positive statement on how service can contribute to identity development. This discussion is designed to clear the air on three points typically found in the literature and popular media. One is that contemporary youth are exceedingly self-interested, marked with an almost unbridled hedonism that needs to be reformed. Another is that contemporary youth are not equipped to take up adult roles in society because they are enclosed in their narrow "youth culture," which runs counter to adult society. And a third is that contemporary youth, more than prior generations in this century, lack political knowledge and, even worse, seem disinterested in taking responsibility for society.

In a review of the film *Kids* that appeared in the *Educational Researcher*, Giroux (1996, 31) describes insightfully the "demonization of youth" in contemporary U.S. society: "[L]auded as a symbol of hope for the future, while scorned as a threat to the existing social order, youth have become objects of ambivalence caught between contradictory discourses and spaces of transition." He supports his point by using examples from recent films that depict adolescents as amoral, anti-intellectual, and dangerous.

In this chapter, we argue that youth have been cast in an undeserved negative light, with service presented as an unrealistic panacea for larger societal problems. Having made this argument, we present a positive case for service by showing how it can be a developmental opportunity that builds upon youth's strengths and their desire to participate as members in society.

Self-Interest

Do youth today manifest excessive self-interest beyond that observed in previous generations? We know of no evidence to support the contention that this generation of young people is abnormally focused on self-satisfaction and lacking in concern or respect for other people. A fact that counters the view of excessive selfishness is that a majority of today's high school students work part-time while they attend school. An annual survey of high school seniors conducted since 1976 indicates that 70% of all seniors work part-time. Although there are differing opinions about the meaning of youth's part-time work (Fine, Mortimer, and Roberts 1990), at a minimum, this work can be seen as taking away from free time and requires youth to adhere to prescribed regimens. While youth work, in part, to provide themselves with power to purchase material goods and entertainment, it is recognized that their work is condoned by parents and contributes to the family by easing some of the financial burden of supplying clothes, funds for entertainment, allowances, and the like. Insofar as parents are parties to youth's work, it is reasonable to view it as part of a consensual system of exchange in which financial responsibility is shared for the family's good.

Data on delinquency provide a second fact that challenges the thesis of excessive self-interest. Siegel and Senna (1994) report that property crime, which is by far the largest category of juvenile crime, has remained stable since 1970. This is not to deny the current problem with youth violence and gun-related crime, which has increased but involves a very small portion of youth. Images of violent crime should not be used to characterize all youth, particularly minority youth, as "superpredators" or as different from previous generations (Giroux 1996; MacLeod 1995; Males 1994). The impression that youth-based crime has recently risen precipitously is neither correct nor novel. For instance, fear of increasing delinquency was manifest during the 1950s when, in fact, crime rates were no higher than in earlier decades (Gilbert 1986). What then accounts for this broad negative impression?

It may be that this negative view of youth reflects adults' own doubts about society. Is it youth who manifest unbridled self-interest or is it adults who, in the commercial and political sectors during the 1980s, violated public trust in the quest for excessive wealth and power? Is it youth who lack moral direction or adults who, for example, fail to meet child-custody agreements or publicly promote racial divisiveness in the name of making government programs more efficient? Numerous violations of public and personal trust are evident to any informed adolescent, and the gap between ideals and actual behavior could easily be a source of embarrassment to adults and confusion to youth (Boyte 1991).

Let us now look at data that positively counteract claims about youth's excessive self-interest and amorality. The findings come from a series of studies on youth's community service. Most of the service reported in these studies was undertaken voluntarily, while an undocumented proportion was part of mandatory school- or community-based programs. Youth's participation in voluntary work, by definition, implies involvement in helping others when youth could otherwise act primarily for their own satisfaction. A first question is, how many youth are actually involved in community service? One estimate comes from a national survey, Monitoring the Future, which has been administered to high school seniors annually since 1976, through the sponsorship of

Table 1.1 Percentages of High School Seniors Who Participate in Community Affairs or Volunteer Work Never, Occasionally, or Frequently, 1976–1992

Responses	1976–77	1978–79	1980–81	1982–83	1984–85	1986–87	1988–89	1991–92
Never	34	31	31	33	31	32	34	33
Occasionally	44	46	46	45	46	45	44	43
Frequently	22	23	23	22	23	23	22	24

Note. Date from Monitoring the Future.

the National Institute on Drug Abuse (see Bachman, Johnston, and O'Malley 1993). Among other things, Monitoring the Future includes the question "During the past year, have you participated in community affairs or volunteer work?" Possible responses are "Never," "A few times," "Monthly," "Weekly," and "Daily." Answers are reported in table 1.1, with "Monthly" to "Daily" collapsed into one category called "Frequently." Results are grouped in adjacent two-year spans, with 1990 data unavailable.

Two findings are notable. (1) About only one-third of the seniors in any year said that they had not participated in service activity, while 22% to 24% said they had participated on a frequent basis, defined here as at least once a month. The remaining seniors said they had participated at least occasionally in the past year. (2) The percentages of students in each category have not changed appreciably since 1976. The rates for no, occasional, and frequent participation remained nearly constant over the 17-year span. The steady rates indicate that youth, as represented by these seniors, have not become either more or less selfish.

A further look at community service comes from a recent Gallup survey in which 389 14- to 17-year-olds nationwide were asked whether they had done volunteer service during the past year, which services they performed, and how they got involved (Hodgkinson and Weitzman 1990). The rate of service participation was 58%, which is similar to that of the combined scores for "Occasionally" and "Frequently" in table 1.1. It was found that students performed a broad array of services that brought them in contact with many sectors and age segments of society. Student services included tutoring other children, baby-sitting, washing cars to raise money for charity, caring for elderly adults, coaching younger children, entertaining institutionalized adults, and working for organized charities. And students said that service opportunities were made available through institutional memberships (churches and schools) and interpersonal relationships (parents and friends who did service with them).

These results are supported by a third study of high school students from Long Island and Ontario (Youniss 1993). About 1,200 students were asked whether they did service on a regular basis during the past year, and what they did. Twenty-eight percent said they did service on a regular basis. This percentage is close to the 22–24% for high school seniors in the "Frequently" category in table 1.1. The service activities that students described were similar to those reported by

Hodgkinson and Weitzman's sample. Students cared for younger children, did chores for ailing neighbors, tutored retarded children, coached younger children in sports, visited patients in hospitals, entertained or visited elderly persons in homes for the aged, assisted at local museums and art galleries, took leadership roles in clubs and organizations for children and peers, and helped raise money for local charities by canvassing and putting on performances.

Although institutional affiliations were not specifically requested, students frequently supplied information that showed again how important institutions were in mediating service and that youth were in contact with these institutions. Service activities were typically done through the aegis of youth organizations such as the Boy Scouts, Girls Club, and 4-H; sports associations; formal charities such as the Heart Fund and Cancer Society; and local churches, schools, hospitals, and residential-care settings. This shows that youth may not be so distant from society as some commentators suggest (Baxley and Lewis 1996; Howard 1996). Numerous organizations exist to serve the needs of people in unfortunate circumstances. Some are formal charities, such as the local Multiple Sclerosis Society and Greenpeace, but many are informal charities run by churches that provide homeless shelters, day-care centers, or food pantries. These institutions support a major portion of the communal side of present society (O'Neill 1994). Each of these organizations is managed by and enlists commitment from numerous adults who are thereby linked to one another through a shared ideology. When youth work for these organizations, they are connected to adults and the ideology and social traditions they represent.

Finally, these data are complemented by national surveys of school-based community service programs (Conrad and Hedin 1982; Newmann and Rutter 1983). Newmann and Rutter (1986) have classified the number and types of programs that are available to students through their high schools. The service activities found in these programs are similar to those reported above and indicate that the pool of talents and energy youth possess are, in fact, put to use not just for themselves but for the benefit of others. These activities bring youth in contact with persons of various ages and social classes and introduce them to ideologies and regimens of formal institutions. Because programs are not uniform in design and quality, it is difficult to offer generalizations about their structure. Nevertheless, these surveys add to the concurring evidence on youth's extensive involvement in service and clearly counter broad claims about this generation's excessive selfishness and distance from societal traditions.

Age Segregation and Youth Culture

The studies just reviewed suggest that lack of youth-adult interaction and segregation of youth in their own culture are exaggerated claims. Part-time work and service experience may give youth meaningful contact with adults and institutions, and provide more intergenerational contact than images of MTV, fast food, and teen fashions suggest. They also offer youth opportunities to experience themselves in the contexts of organizational regimens and ideologies. These results, therefore, already go a long way in countering the second claim about contemporary youth.

James Coleman (1961) is credited with documenting the postwar emergence of a "youth culture" through a study of ten Midwestern high schools. He noted that the most admired students in these schools were not high academic achievers, but cheerleaders and athletes. He interpreted this as a sign that youth as a group were diverging from traditional adult values.

The data on teenage valuations of crowds are not, however, simple and require further analysis. Studies of high schools in various parts of the United States show that within the so-called youth culture, adolescents themselves distinguish a variety of groups according to their dominant behavior and values. Brown (1990), Eckert (1989), and others report that adolescents differentiate a range of crowds whose values correspond to the array one would find among adults. In addition to cheerleaders and athletes, students identify crowds oriented to a range of interests from academic achievement, at one end, to drugs, at the other end. Further, within the most popular group, some students also claim to be oriented to academic achievement, placing themselves in two categories at once, for example, sports and studies.

Caution must be used when trying to characterize an entire cohort of teenagers. While Coleman insightfully noted the emergence of unique cultural forms that distinguished youth from adult culture, it should not be overlooked that variations among youth cover a range that parallels types found among adults (Fasick 1984). Moreover, incidences of scholar-athletes and scholar-partygoers indicate that youth can manage membership in peer culture without abandoning adult-endorsed orientations as signified, for example, by academic achievement (Rigsby and McDill 1975; Youniss, Yates, and Su in press).

The overlap between youth and adult values is shown not only in peer crowds but also in the quality of relationships between youth and their families. The social science literature supports the argument that the majority of youth are strongly attached to and respect their parents and families. There is a continuous line of research over three decades that supports this proposition. The series began with a report by Douvan and Adelson (1966) on Midwestern high school students who were sampled in the mid-1950s. These adolescents cared about their parents, trusted and respected them, and found relations with them not particularly conflictual. Comparable findings have come subsequently from adolescents in states on the East Coast (Kandel and Lesser 1972), the Midwest (Offer, Ostrov, and Howard 1981); the mid-Atlantic region (Youniss and Smollar 1985), and the West Coast (Steinberg, Elmen, and Mounts 1989).

Insofar as regular interaction between teenagers and parents implies exposure to adult norms, it seems reasonable to conclude that the majority of adolescents have practical experience with the norms and values adult society espouses. This conclusion is bolstered by a parallel set of findings that offer a fresh look at peer relations as a complement to youth's relationships with parents. Contrary to the popular equation of peers as sources of deviancy from societal norms, there is a literature showing that peer relationships are principled and demanding of the practice of traditional moral norms. For example, studies indicate that, as a matter of course, friendship demands the practice of cooperation, is sustained through the principle of fairness, requires dealings with conflict, and leads to maintenance of mutual understanding (Berndt 1982; Youniss and Smollar 1985).

This is not to idealize peer relationships, which obviously are as conflict-laden as any other interpersonal relationship. Rather, the purpose is to show that, even though youth spend time with peers, they should not be construed as moving deeper into an antinormative abyss. Although some aspects of the peer world may foster such a movement, the core relationship of friendship is inherently conducive to reinforcing prosocial norms, which are sources of social capital. This point is reinforced by the finding that adolescents tend to view their relationships with parents and with friends as different but compatible, rather than tension-ridden from having to manage opposing values (e.g., Sebald 1986). Fasick (1984) offers insight on this issue by noting that many youth desire to emulate their parents, who appear to them as successful and leading lives adolescents themselves would like to repeat. Youth in groups that share a positive orientation toward parents most likely practice norms with each other that are similar to the norms they practice with parents, with appropriate accommodations.

Political and Moral Awareness

The recent surge in calls for service also has roots in the perception that contemporary youth seem politically apathetic and morally rudderless (Conrad and Hedin 1991). Many private and several public high schools have mandated specified hours of community service for graduation. Detroit, Minneapolis, Atlanta, and Los Angeles have such initiatives. Maryland now requires 72 hours of service of its high school graduates, and Vermont and Pennsylvania are weighing similar laws. In 1990, Congress passed the National and Community Service Act and, in 1993, the National and Community Service Trust Act, which have the objective of increasing service participation by youth (Boyte 1991; Kahne and Westheimer 1996).

How strong is the case that youth lack political interest and moral fortitude? The findings from a study of youth's attitudes toward citizenship published by the People for the American Way (1989) have been used by service advocates (e.g., Lewis 1992) to support the contention that contemporary youth feel politically uninvolved. The sample consisted of 1,006 youth between the ages 15 and 24, of whom 96% said they had helped or would help an elderly neighbor, 95% said they had helped or would help a friend with a drug problem, but only 36% said they had worked or would work in a political campaign (15). The majority of the sample, 68%, highly valued a "close-knit family life" (15), and 43% said that helping others in need defined "good citizenship" (30). At the same time, youth did not view themselves as having political potency. For instance, 70% said that "[s]ometimes politics and government seem so complicated that a person like me can't really understand what's going on" (31), and only 12% equated good citizenship with voting and involvement in politics (30). The study also reports the perception of both youth and teachers that contemporary youth are less involved and politically interested than youth a decade ago.

Returning to the annual Monitoring the Future survey of high

Table 1.2 Actual and Projected Political Involvement of High School Seniors (percentages)

Type of Involvement	1976–77	1978–79	1980–81	1982–83	1984–85	1986–87	1988–89	1991–92
Voted	7	5	6	4	7	4	9	7
Likely to vote	81	83	83	83	83	84	80	79
Boycotted	9	7	7	5	4	5	4	8
Likely to boycott	23	22	22	15	13	13	16	23
Demonstrated	4	3	4	3	3	3	3	4
Likely to demonstrate	17	17	18	17	15	15	18	23

Note. Data from Monitoring the Future.

school seniors, we suggest that youth's actual and projected political behavior may not be a cause for alarm. Table 1.2 reports results for three indicators of political attitudes: having already or being likely to vote, to "boycott certain products or stores," or to "participate in lawful demonstrations."

These results give no credence to claims that today's youth lack political interest or represent a downward trend in political interest and behavior. The proportions of seniors who have or are likely to participate in these various kinds of political actions have changed little from 1976 to 1993, indicating a fairly steady relationship between youth and the political realm. Even patterns have remained steady; for instance, actual voting by seniors, expressed as raw percentages or percentages of eligible 18-year-olds, rises during presidential election years, declines in off years, then picks up again at the next presidential election. This pattern has held steady from 1976 to 1992.

We are unaware of comparable historical data that can answer questions about this generation's moral posture relative to preceding generations. But the data presented in table 1.1 for community service and the studies that followed demonstrate a steady tendency for the majority of high school students to value this brand of altruism.

Recent collected volumes on current research in moral development make no note of a decline or problem in youth's moral reasoning or behavior (Killen and Hart, 1995; Kurtines and Gewirtz 1995). Further, in a unique study by Walker, de Vries, and Trevethan (1987), mother-father-youth triads were assessed on hypothetical and real-life moral dilemmas, youth scored according to expected norms, showing normal moral maturity for their age. They did not differ in style from their parents, but seemed on paths that would lead to achieving the levels their parents had reached.

Perhaps it is worth recalling here the well-known series of studies from Yale University by Hartshorne, May, and Maller (1929). In the late 1920s, these studies caused alarm when youth were found to be moral relativists who would not cheat if adults were watching but who would cheat if they thought they were unobserved. This kind of result led the authors to fault the notion of moral character and replace it with a utilitarian situational morality. But note that this cohort of youth proved not to be morally deficient but went on to manage the World War II effort and, after the war, rebuilt the country's economy and helped make massive advances in civil rights, education, and national social programs.

Summary

In this section, we have argued that there are exaggerated concerns about contemporary youth's self-interest, values, and attitudes and that a case for increasing community service participation should not be made as a way of overcoming youth's perceived deficits. We believe that a stronger approach is to view service as a developmental opportunity that draws upon youth's preexisting strengths and their desire to be meaningfully involved in society.

A Sounder Justification for Community Service

In the remainder of this chapter, a positive case is made for community service by combining the documented strengths of youth with an analysis of youth's relationships to society. We begin by reviewing William James's 1909 essay, which is still used to justify service programs for youth. We compare the social conditions to which he was responding with contemporary social conditions. We argue that community service may rectify the problematic relationship between youth and society, which is more a function of institutional structures than of deficiencies in youth. A clear picture of these relationships ought to provide a sound groundwork for constructing better service programs.

James Revisited

James's 1909 essay was addressed to America's elite youth, the nation's future leaders. According to James, Western culture had used war as a means to organize and give discipline to society. The process of making war demanded that resources be concertedly directed and conserved. This entailed group discipline and sacrifice, which, in turn, enhanced patriotism, collective pride, and shared honor. James wondered aloud whether a nation could achieve these same outcomes by substituting a moral crusade for a military cause. He knew this was a utopian ideal, but he feared that in a time of peace, there was likely to be a drift to a "simple pleasure economy" ([1909] 1971, 12).

He pictured an antidote in which young men would be conscripted into a moral army to fight "injustice" so that a sense of community and the common good would be restored. James, who taught at Harvard University, noted that the elite young men of his day lacked the military ideals of "hardihood and discipline" and were about to assume leadership in "the luxurious classes," which had become "blind to" the lot of the less fortunate classes (13). He therefore proposed an army of "haves" that would be sent

> [t]o coal and iron mines, to freight trains, to fishing fleets in December, to dish washing, clothes-washing, and window-washing, to road-building and tunnel-making, to foundries and stoke-holes, and to the frames of skyscrapers [thus] would our gilded youth . . . get the childishness knocked out of them, and . . . come back into society with healthier sympathies and soberer ideas. They would have paid their blood-tax, done their own part in the immemorial human warfare against nature; they would tread the earth more proudly, the women would value them more highly, they would be better fathers and teachers of the following generation. (14)

It is worth comparing the societal conditions that stimulated James's vision to the conditions that prevail today and probably stand behind the call for community service. (1) There is again a perceived split between classes, between the "haves" of the youth cohort who attend college and the "have-nots" who enter the labor market immediately after high school (*Forgotten half* 1988). This class split has been exacerbated by a widening income gap between the wealthy and the poor (Holmes 1996; Rich 1994). (2) A military draft seems as distant today as it was in James's day. This has led to a peacetime outlook, which to James could bode lack of seriousness and overinvestment in a pleasure orientation. (3) As in the first decade of the century, the United States is again experiencing burgeoning immigration, which puts pressure on the labor market and threatens to undo cultural and value consensus. (4) The labor market itself is undergoing drastic change; whereas 85 years ago major corporations were being formed and manufacturing jobs were expanding, corporations today are being restructured and manufacturing jobs are being exported and reduced for the purpose of greater efficiency.

It may not be incidental that these parallel conditions coincide with a call to put youth back in touch with the real workings of society. In contrast to James's day, however, there is an added problem for which service seems an appropriate solution. Today's youth appear to be excluded from many of the central activities of society. From a historical perspective, youth as a whole lack contact due to the societal expectation of age segregation, which is symbolized in the separate spheres of school and work for youth and adults, respectively. This creation of the modern era contrasts with the past when youth were socialized as they participated with adults in family subsistence labor. In the late nineteenth century, however, youth began to be squeezed out of the workforce and shunted to schools, which restricted their interactions with adults, limiting them primarily to the peer domain (Gillis 1981; Kett 1977). A concern with the problem of age segregation has stimulated some social scientists in recent years to reinvestigate the apprenticeship system and to look comparatively at other countries such as Germany that still utilize this system (Hamilton 1990).

Youth's distance from the workings of society is coupled with population diversity that challenges the maintenance of the country's cultural consensus on norms and values. The resulting diffusion is as true of youth in one socioeconomic class as in another. More-elite classes of youth are likely to have interaction with normative adults but lack experience with youth from other classes (Fasick 1984). At the same time, residential segregation has resulted in new immigrant youth's having closest interactions with minority youth whose cultural outlook is most likely to differ from mainstream culture (Massey and Denton 1993).

Coleman's later work (1987; see also Coleman and Hoffer 1987), which used the concept of *social capital,* offers one approach to understanding the impact of youth-adult separation coupled with cultural diffusion and class segregation. He argued that there was an identifiable set of standards and values that are normative for mainstream adults in our society. Individuals who know and abide by them have the social equivalent of capital, which allows them to act effectively in society. Coleman believed that youth accrue social capital by interacting with norm-bearing adults because interactions are predicated on these norms and values. To the degree that youth lack contact with normative adults, they lack opportunities for acquiring capital that enables them to take on adult roles in normative society.

Making History, Not Just Living the Moment

The similarity of present conditions to those James saw, and the distancing of youth from society as well as from peers in other social classes, may account for some of the specific proposals found in the current service literature. We end this chapter by outlining views presented by scholars in sociology, education, and psychology who offer rationales for service that address the relationship between youth and society.

Boyte (1991), a sociologist, has distinguished between two rationales, one based on "care" and the other promoting "participation." He argues that the motive of producing a "feel-good" sense of caring for others is insufficient grounds for service. Boyte finds "disingenuous" the argument that youth need to put concern for others ahead of their self-interest in a society "that glorifies 'lifestyles of the rich and famous' and praises the virtues of free enterprise" (766). Boyte's counterproposal is that service ought to be designed for youth to experience participation in a "problem-solving politic" (767).

Educators Kahne and Westheimer (1996) also point to the importance of differentiating between an approach to service that emphasizes charity and maintaining the status quo and one that emphasizes justice and social change. They propose that policy makers have not clearly distinguished the goals of positive feelings toward self and others from the tension of learning how difficult, yet energizing, it is to participate in political process and moral restructuring. When this distinction is made, the kinds of programs one designs and the sorts of outcomes one expects take certain shape.

For these authors, service is a means to form citizens who understand the struggle and rewards, energy and exhilaration, that make up the actual political process. They speculate that service can stimulate youth to use their new cognitive capacities to reflect on their performances in socially meaningful situations. They want service to nurture the development of individuals who will make history and not simply try to draw as much personal gain from society as present conditions will allow.

Finally, Logan (1985), a psychologist, uses Erikson's framework to elucidate the potential role of service in youth. Erikson predicates identity development on a prior sense of *industry* through which individuals experience themselves as actors capable of meeting goals through performance. When identity concerns subsequently loom, adolescents test themselves primarily through action and performance. The developmental process is thwarted, however, when youth cannot actually test themselves in a societal context that allows evaluation of their performance.

Logan notes that productive work and its equivalents would be a logical locus for identity testing. But in contemporary society, this avenue is often blocked as youth are directed away from productive labor and forced to deal with ersatz forms. Logan suggests that, in the absence of experiencing the effects of their labor, youth might even seek substitutes through artificial stimulants and physical routines that produce feelings of exhilaration, fatigue, and satisfaction. These effects that youth seek may be compensatory for an identity process that is limited to the "existential" realm when testing by performance is blocked.

Logan suggests that community service that consists in using one's talents to affect other people's lives would allow youth to assess their identities through action. Such service would provide youth with clear feedback on whether their actions are effective. This proposal takes identity out of the purely existential domain and permits youth to appraise themselves as producers rather than just consumers. In so acting, youth also have access to adult society in ways that make social verification possible. Not just oneself or peers but also adults can judge whether youth's actions have helped transform the aspect of society to which the service was directed. Consequently, the barriers that segregate youth are broken down, and the identity process is extended into adult society where it can be informed by tradition, history, and ideology (Erikson 1968).

Conclusion

It is very difficult to characterize contemporary youth as having one kind of relationship to society. The social science data have offered mixed findings, and adolescents compose a diverse group who differ, among other ways, in cultural and socioeconomic backgrounds. However, we do think that there are structural impediments that keep youth from participating meaningfully in society. These impediments are manifest in the way that societal activities are often segregated by age, class, race, and culture. We wish to stress that the evidence we do have shows that, when given the opportunity to engage in activities such as community service, youth participate with enthusiasm and commitment (e.g., Hodgkinson and Weitzman 1990).

The views presented at the end of this chapter by Boyte, Kahne and Westheimer, and Logan suggest how service can serve as a productive developmental experience for contemporary youth. Service can provide opportunities for youth to be taken seriously as contributing members to society and to participate in meaningful, problem-solving actions. In accounting for the impact of service on youth, Logan suggests that service encourages a productive sense of industry, and Kahne and Westheimer speculate that certain types of service stimulate reflection on society's workings and political processes. In chapter 2, we take up the question of how service affects youth's political-moral development. We outline a theory on the relationship between service and identity development in adolescents.

CHAPTER TWO

Social-Historical Identity: A Theoretical Framework for Service

In studying individuals who were recognized for lifetimes of outstanding moral commitment, Colby and Damon (1992) concluded that these people did not consider themselves unusual or heroic, because moral action had become so deeply ingrained in their self-understanding. Even though they expended extraordinary efforts to help others, they viewed their actions as ordinary in the sense of being normal and integrated into their working assumptions about self and reality. No meaningful distinction could be made between their moral outlooks and their personalities (cf. Hart et al. 1995). If it were asked whether morality or identity had priority for them, the answer would be that the two had become too intertwined to be differentiated (Davidson and Youniss 1991).

This result provides a starting point for framing a developmental outlook on community service. There must be developmental precursors to an adulthood in which morality has become central to an individual's self-perception. Since adolescence is a time when the identity process becomes focal, it is reasonable to look to it for signs of adults' formation. For Erikson (1968), there are two complementary and essential aspects to the adolescent identity process. *Personal identity* involves reflecting on one's talents, weaknesses, and proclivities, in order to form a clear sense of sameness and continuity across varied experiences. In complement, Erikson uses the term *ego identity* to refer to one's relationships to other persons and to a social-historical context (50). For clarity, we will use the term *social identity*.

Community service applies to both aspects of this process. It engages adolescents' talents by requiring active extension of self into the world via performance. This follows logically from the preceding stage of industry and provides the adolescent with concrete feedback for self-reflective clarification. Because service brings adolescents into contact with the workings of society, it also provides opportunities for reflection on society's political, moral, and historical dimensions. To paraphrase Flacks (1988), service may be an occasion for adolescents to experience themselves as makers of history by providing meaning beyond the mere accommodation of their lives in passive compliance to society.

Erikson as a Social Theorist

Erikson's 1950 book, *Childhood and Society*, gave new definition to the concept of identity. The concept was picked up by therapists who viewed it as an alternative to the psychoanalytic notion of ego development without having that theory's many encumbrances. The concept was largely confined to professional circles until the 1960s, when the baby-boom cohort reached adolescence and expressed itself through public protests regarding free speech, military intervention in Southeast Asia, authority on college campuses, and the like. Whereas immediately preceding generations of youth had been involved in the nation's World War II effort and postwar normalization, the 1960 youth cohort broke the pattern with public displays that challenged cherished social conventions and institutions. Youth made it clear that they were not going to sit on the sidelines cheering tradition on, but would take a direct hand in reforming politics and public morality.

In a search for understanding these intense expressions of anger, enthusiasm, and energy, scholars and practitioners found relevance in the concept of identity. Even Erikson was surprised at the fascination the concept had engendered when, near the end of the decade, he looked back and saw that identity had become "the pet subject of the *americankanische Populaerpsychologie*" (1968, 16).

The concept was sufficiently general to admit of diverse interpretations. "Identity search" was put to many uses, including justifying youth's rebellion as a developmental imperative, describing youth's idealism, and explaining how youth's enthusiasms could quickly turn to Fascist intolerance. Most commentators have focused on the inner dynamics of personal identity, with emphasis on the internal struggle to find authentic and satisfying self-definition. This outlook fit the times when individuals sought inner sanctuary from crises in government institutions, shifts in norms for marriage, changing roles for women and men, and so on. If society was in flux, how could youth form stable identities and gain a sense of continuity that could be projected into the future?

While Erikson addressed the personal side in a compelling way, and even perhaps because he addressed it so well, the social side of identity was neglected by researchers. It is a given that adolescents seek to unify past with anticipated future experiences; what needs to be added is that adolescents also seek to integrate themselves into society's history (Grotevant 1993; Hogan and Emler 1995). They need to feel "solidification" with the culture (Gergen and Gergen 1983, 256), or an "inner solidarity with a group's ideals and identity" (Erikson 1958, 109). As youth focus inwardly to find self-sameness, they must also look outward to form relationships with society's traditions. This neglected aspect of placing oneself in a social-historical context will now be discussed in detail.

Erikson's Identity: Youth and Crisis

At the height of the 1960s student unrest, Erikson was invited to assemble a group of his essays on identity. In preparing the book, *Identity: Youth and Crisis* (1968), Erikson wrote a prologue that offered an extensive analysis of the societal side of identity. He proposed that society was responsible for providing youth with clear symbols that spelled out its traditions and organized its history. He called these symbols ideologies, which youth could either accept or reject, but which they needed to consider in order to make their options clear. These symbols also served as rallying points for enlisting youth's commitment to ideals that were worth caring about, criticizing, or renewing. Erikson believed that the eruption of discontent and protest was as much due to shortcomings in society's leaders who did not provide these mobilizing symbols, as to youth's inherent imperative to question the older generation.

Erikson (1968) proposed that identity is a generational issue. As adolescents seek "a tangible collective future" (49), the older generation's role is to provide them with ideals that signify a hopeful future. Instead of being focused primarily on the question "Who am I?" youth are concerned about the society they will inherit and have to decide how they can best relate to it. Interest in society is essential if youth are to honor a particular version of history and work toward a future that merits their commitment.

Adolescents need to become part of a larger collective that transcends the self's personal biography. This collective has a history and can be projected into the future. Erikson illustrated this meaning of transcendence with a quotation from Freud, who called his deepest identity "the safe privacy of a common mental construction . . . my Jewish nature" (20). This shows that the inner individual and communal culture are reciprocal terms within identity. In Erikson's terms, the two "define each other and are truly relative to each other" (23).

This point was made forcefully in Erikson's biographies of Luther (1958) and Gandhi (1969). Because of the heroic character of these individuals, it is sometimes forgotten that all people face the problem of transcending specific experience to find social-historical meaning for themselves. In this task, individuals need to look beyond the boundaries of personal experience for collective realities with which a worthwhile identification can be made.

Ideology

In describing society, Erikson repeatedly uses the term *ideology*, which unfortunately has negative connotation in psychology. What does Erikson mean by this term? Ideology denotes "a universal psychological need for a system of ideas that provides a convincing world image" (1968, 31). Contemporary society encompasses an array of diverse viewpoints and values. Society needs to be segmented so that youth can make clear choices from the many available options. Ideology reduces the array to a limited range. Erikson cites as traditional sources of ideology economic theory, religion, political beliefs, geographic attachments, and ethnic affiliation. Today's options also include ideologies of technological possibilities, ecological prospects, and new forms of humanism that borrow from traditional religion (Luckmann 1991).

Erikson sees ideology as a means for adolescents to simplify and organize their experience. Experience via everyday interactions has the potential to be scattered into discrete events. When preceded by an ideological outlook, however, "a million daily tasks and transactions fall into practical patterns and spontaneous ritualization which can be shared by leaders and led, men and women, adults and children" (32). In this way, ideology provides the social glue that allows identity to transcend individuality and become synthesized within a collective.

In the 1968 book, Erikson's essay on the life of George Bernard Shaw further illustrates the point that identity and ideology are complementary. Ideology precedes identity in giving youth a means for organizing experience. And as ideology and identity become synthesized, individuals are linked in a common identification that allows shared understanding at a higher level. Erikson argues that youth want to share ideals with others so that they can join in historical realities from which these ideals sprang. By identifying with ideologies, youth become distinguished as members of particular groups, and this gives them ego strength they could not acquire on their own, no matter how authentic these isolated individuals may be.

Industry and "Making History"

Erikson recognized that, in modern societies, children often cannot participate in the productive economy of family life or larger society. They practice productivity indirectly through school performances that prepare them for adult roles in our postindustrial culture. Schooling is necessarily general so that it can provide broad education for a wide number of possible careers. Noting the obvious problems this kind of culture spawns, Erikson proposed that *industry* is critical to development. Children need to learn how to perform and achieve cooperatively with others, if they are to enter into the culture. This lesson has lasting implications, then, as adults need to cooperate to sustain a democratic society.

The role of achievement in social identity is illustrated in adolescents' belief that society's leaders have actually earned their positions by being the best at what they do. Not chance, but concerted effort gained them leadership positions. To think otherwise might lead to cynicism. Thus, youth tend to believe that leaders merit their positions, and this motivates them to succeed, as a societal ethos is incorporated into the self and gives youth "rejuvenative power" (134). This does not mean that adolescents support, for example, political leaders unquestioningly and are not sometimes disappointed by political processes (Flanagan and Gallay 1995). Rather, adolescents need to believe that, in principle, deeds brought individuals to leadership and that youth, through their own deeds, will ascend to their rightful leadership roles in the next generation.

Social identity, in contrast to personal identity, is based on employing one's agency collaboratively in constructing a better world. Choosing an ideology and working to bring it to fruition flows from industry and moves the identity process ahead. Erikson stressed youth's role in social evolution, as youth expend their "loyalties and energies both to the conservation of that which continues to feel true and to the revolutionary correction of that which has lost its regenerative significance" (134).

A Grounded Idealism

Erikson realized that even in collective agreement there was a risk of ideological divisiveness. For every collective linkage, there is a risk of exclusion of some other group. Any ideology can become a means for a group identity that creates social division and threatens broader unity. The antidote is communication across groups and between generations, when each seeks humanity's evolution.

Erikson ultimately trusts each generation's ability to move toward a nonexclusionary society. The vehicle is "an adult ethics [to] guarantee to the next generation an equal chance to experience the full cycle of humanness . . . this alone permits the individual to transcend his identity—to become as truly individual as he will ever be, and as truly beyond all individuality" (41).

Although idealistic, Erikson's confidence in social evolution is grounded in three principles. (1) Identity is based on *industry;* the individual has the ability to act as an intelligent agent and is able to design action for explicit goals. (2) Identity advances through joint verification or *social relatedness* wherein individuals, with trust, look to others for cooperative feedback and understanding. (3) The identity process is guided by *ethical considerations.* While each individual needs identifying ideologies, all individuals can move beyond self- or group interest to reach common understanding. When people transcend such divisions, they can move to a common humanity that treats individual and group differences in morally just ways.

Community Service and Developing Identity

The remainder of this chapter illustrates how Erikson's ideas help to explain empirical findings on the effects of service. We previously reviewed several studies on community service (Yates and Youniss 1996b), and will now focus on data that inform our theoretical position. The work bears on the three core principles of identity: agency, social relatedness, and political-moral understanding.

Agency and Industry

Erikson predicates social identity on industry, or being able to achieve desired outcomes through one's actions. Actions that count have effects on the social domain and allow the individual to sustain relationships with other persons and social institutions. Anything less would leave the individual in an existential state broaching egoism.

Potential problems stand in the way of seeing how opportunities for actions that encourage a sense of agency are available to contemporary youth. One is the putative age segregation that confines youth to peer culture and keeps them separated from adult society. We argued in chapter 1 that this separation is more a function of how society is construed than a necessary reality that all youth face. Three points help clarify this argument. First, society need not be viewed as a set of preexisting structures but may be seen as constituted through people's everyday interactions. Second, the putative boundary between peer and adult cultures may be less distinct than commentators have suggested. Studies show that peer and adult cultures develop together from early childhood and that most adolescents live within both domains quite adaptively. Third, political and moral agency consists in actions that need not be heroic, but are of an everyday nature and are readily available to youth (Colby and Damon 1995; Flanagan and Gallay 1995).

Society and interpersonal interaction. The definition of society as a creation of interactions of individuals is central to a genre of thinking called microsociology (e.g., Collins 1979; Giddens 1993; Corsaro and Eder 1990). Giddens (1993, 4, 5), for example, rejects the dualism of "the individual and society" and replaces it with *reproduced practices,* which presume individuals are agents whose actions emanate from self, collectivities, and social organizations. One need not choose between macro- and microrealities, because both exist in fact. Although real, macrostructures depend for existence on micropractices that constitute them. For example, there is no democratic society unless people practice democracy.

Individuals' actions are not determined in any hard sense by macrostructures. Such structures restrict or enable particular kinds of actions, but do not eliminate the need for individuals with the capacities for reflectivity and conscious intention. Individuals can think about structures as they try to maintain or seek to change them. "While not made by any single person, society is created and recreated afresh, if not *ex nihilo,* by the participants in every social encounter. *The production of society* is a skilled performance, sustained and 'made to happen' by human beings" (Giddens 1993, 20).

Collins (1979, 60) distinguishes two ways in which culture is reproduced, through "culture-producing organizations" such as churches or the media, for instance, and through "everyday interactions" or activities that go on all the time at work, at home, and in recreation. Individuals generate theories about society, and their actions follow from these theories. Because people can talk about their theories, conversation is a tool for effecting social change. People exchange views, argue, and convince one another, so in the process they affect mutual understanding of what society is and how it can be altered (Gamson 1992).

Peers and adults. Corsaro and Eder (1990) show that interactions with peers and adults are grounds for the development of adolescents' social understanding. Children's social interactions collectively lead to shared knowledge equivalent to a "culture." Corsaro (1985) describes three characteristics of this culture: themes, rules, and mutual understanding. Children in nursery school established mutually understood *themes* that were continuing topics of daily interactions. Corsaro reports that play, for example, was ordered around themes of "lost-and-found," "danger-rescue," and "death-rebirth."

Second, children interacted according to shared *rules* whose authoritative status depended on joint recognition of violations and agreement to correct them. Third, themes and rules were *mutually understood* by the children, who assigned shared meaning to actions. Members of this culture shared understandings that outsiders could not have comprehended.

Corsaro and Eder note that, while children form peer culture, they simultaneously live in and construct a culture with parents and other adults. Peers in schools and adults in families represent intersecting domains between which social knowledge flows. Parts of each culture flow into the other and reappear in forms appropriate to it (Toren 1993). For instance, age and intelligence originate as values with adults, but later appear in peer culture where children use them for strategic gain—for example, "I'm bigger than you" or "She's smarter than her."

Peer culture does not suddenly loom up at adolescence pitted against adult norms. Children have coexisted in the two domains during their development, with ideas, rules, and moral stances continuously crossing between them. By adolescence, peer and adult spheres are clearly delineated, but also begin to be integrated. Youth need to learn how to translate rules and ethics from one sphere to the other in a two-way process (Youniss and Smollar 1985). Hence, children's social knowledge is not an internalized version of adults' ideas, but is constructed by interacting with adults and by reformulating ideas in interactions with peers, and vice versa.

Political-moral actions. In which actions does adult agency in political and moral domains consist? Flacks (1988) lists political behaviors such as voting, joining special-interest organizations, discussing political issues, working to protect local communities, and changing environmental conditions for health and safety. There are thousands of such actions that adults typically take collectively. These actions, which make history, are the same as those that Giddens, Collins, and others have said go into constituting society. Such actions count because they determine political outcomes, such as elections of local boards, and determine how people perceive the society in which they live. These perceptions, in turn, become grounds for actions because they motivate individuals to collective behavior they might not otherwise pursue.

This kind of agency is a basis for social responsibility. If individuals did not believe their actions counted, they would not feel responsible to register new voters, boycott, strike, march, argue politics, or join movements. Adults do these things because they believe democratic society depends on people acting democratically. It is important that the behaviors that make up adult agency are not extraordinary and have incipient forms in the repertoire of youth.

Flacks's view (1988, 35) that "[o]ur culture provides very weak motivational bases for political participation . . . [while] the strongest motivational structures developed in our culture are those that energize people toward private life and personal fulfillment" may be too pessimistic. It needs to be balanced by the fact that skills required for participation are available to youth and can be fostered through community service and other means. Flacks acknowledges this by defining "democratic culture" as one that "would socialize all its young to feel competent for public participation by providing both the specific skills necessary for public awareness and discourse and a subjective sense of individual self-worth and effectiveness" (35).

Major impediments to the development of agency in youth can be overcome with a proper definition of society, a realization that peer culture is not like a foreign body that enters youth stealthily, poisoning them against adult norms, and awareness that mature agency requires skills that are readily available to youth. We offer this argument not as a final statement but in order to establish clear and reasonable grounds for the proposal that community service can engender a sense of agency that may be developed in the making of competent democratic adults.

Social Relatedness

Erikson (1968) argues that location of self in a social-historical context is essential to identity development, but offers only vague leads about the processes that lead to social integration. Several researchers have noted the importance of membership in organizations that bring youth in contact with adult values and allow them to experience the regimen of organizational rules (Hanks and Eckland 1978; Otto 1976; Ladewig and Thomas 1987; Larson 1994). Organizations such as the Boy or Girl Scouts, hobby clubs, and extracurricular activities may have a socially integrative function. These organizations represent explicit ideologies and set standards for continued membership. They foster engagement with peers, one's parents, and a variety of adults such as coaches, leaders, fans, and fellow hobbyists.

Larson (1994) reported that participation in extracurricular activities had positive benefits during the adolescent era. He studied two groups of students at two-year intervals over a four-year period. One group was first observed prior to junior high school, and the other group was first observed at the start of junior high school. Two consistent results were obtained. Membership in youth organizations at the start of the study predicted membership two and four years later. Second, membership in youth organizations at the start of senior high school was negatively correlated with self-reported delinquency two years later. These findings suggest that belonging to groups with a clear ideology and definite standards of conduct encourages further group membership. In turn, continued membership deters antisocial behavior.

Hanks and Eckland (1978) reported that organizational membership by youth had positive effects that persisted over a 15-year period. They capitalized on a survey given to high school sophomores in 97 schools in 1955 by the Educational Testing Service. Students reported the number and types of organizations in which they were involved.

The list included school publications, debate and political clubs, social-service and religious groups, academic societies, drama or music groups, student government, and science clubs or projects.

Alumni from 42 of the schools were sent another survey in 1970 when they were 30 years old. Of 4,151 alumni surveyed, 2,077 (50%) responded, which yielded a final sample of 916 males and 911 females. These adults stated whether they were currently members, active participants, or leaders in associations categorized as service (e.g., Rotary Club), youth service (e.g., Scouts, Little League), union or trade, political, educational, church-related, community or social action, and organized volunteer work. In addition the alumni described their current political activities and attitudes, including voting behavior and feelings toward government (e.g., "People like me don't have any say about what government does").

The 1955 data were used to predict 1970 adult behavior. The best predictor of membership in organizations at age 30 was membership in youth organizations 15 years previously. It was also found that the best predictor of voting behavior and of alienation was current (1970) organizational membership. In sum, membership in youth organizations predicted membership in adult organizations 15 years later, and membership in organizations at age 30 positively predicted voting behavior and negatively predicted feelings of alienation.

The authors proposed that extracurricular activities have gone unrecognized as important parts of adolescent education. Youth organizations put adolescents in contact with normative adults and peers and encourage the use and development of social and political skills. These skills allow adolescents to become integrated into the surrounding culture and to test themselves as organizational members. These results were essentially the same as those reported by Otto (1976), who found that membership in organizations during high school predicted adult social relatedness and political behavior.

Ladewig and Thomas (1987) provide another example with their 1985 national survey of former members of 4-H clubs, which are sponsored by the U.S. Department of Agriculture to help youth in rural areas assimilate agricultural science into their educational experiences. In 1944, 4-H was extended to urban youth, and in 1985, it reached 1.6 million youth in year-round programs, 1 million more youth in targeted projects, and 1.8 million youth through school curricula.

The 1985 survey was administered to adults in four regions of the country, and a weighted sample of 16,292 adults was asked to list the youth groups to which they had belonged. Of the total, 4,361 had been in no group, 1,638 had been in 4-H, and 10,293 had belonged to other youth organizations (e.g., Scouts, YM/YWCA, Boys or Girls Club, church groups). The mean ages of adults composing these three groups were 51, 42, and 43 years, respectively. Respondents recalled aspects of their membership such as activities they did, the kind of leadership they had, and types of satisfaction they felt. They also listed their current organizational memberships, intensity of involvement, and whether they held leadership positions.

A majority of adults recalled that their youth activities in 4-H and other organizations were challenging, 50% said they had been involved in community-service projects, and 60% recalled they had participated in contests, fairs, debates, or fashion shows. Adults recalled that these projects were "useful" and "challenging," made a "contribution," and helped them develop skills and social responsibility.

The authors reported two long-term effects akin to those reported by Hanks and Eckland and Otto. First, alumni of 4-H and other youth organizations, more often than organizational nonmembers, said that their own children were currently members of youth groups. The respective percentages were 45%, 44%, and 31%. Second, current active membership or leadership in normative organizations was considerably higher for adults who had belonged to youth organizations. Current organizations included civic clubs, chambers of commerce, committees involved in community affairs, agricultural groups, political organizations, community organizing groups, and church groups. Alumni from 4-H or other youth groups were at least twice as likely to be currently active in organizations as were adults who did not belong to youth groups. Alumni of 4-H and other youth groups were even more likely to hold leadership offices in organizations currently than were nonjoiners.

In summary, results from these studies indicate that early engagement in social organizations and organized activities is associated with long-term engagement even into midlife. Social relatedness seems to become part of what the individual does and, interestingly, carries over to what offspring do in their youth. Some of the early organized activity qualifies as service to one's community either in practice, ideology, or both (e.g., 4-H). Some of the adult behavior qualifies as reproducing community (e.g., participating in civic organizations). The linking process seems to be social relatedness, which combines Erikson's features of ideological clarity and collective identity.

Political-Moral Identity

Two studies on service during the 1950s and 1960s civil rights era provide evidence that connects political and moral activities during youth with long-range political and moral outlooks. Each looked at a specific group of youth who worked in the South registering Black voters, teaching Black children in Freedom Schools, and demonstrating through sit-ins and other protest activities. Both studies provide data at the time students participated and 20 or more years later. Each study also offers data, for both time points, from comparison groups of peers who had not participated in these activities when they were students.

McAdam (1988) describes the political climate in the South which led to Freedom Summer 1964. Whereas the nation had experienced 20 years of economic growth, the Black population in the state of Mississippi remained locked in Depression-era lack of opportunity. While the gross national product had risen an average of 6.5% per year since 1946, the majority of Mississippi Blacks lived in "grinding poverty," with one in three employed in handpicking of cotton and 86% living below the federal standard for poverty. With only 6.7% of eligible Black voters registered, a number of local and national groups tried to alter their state of political impotency. Among others, the Student Nonviolent Coordinating Committee (SNCC), which was formed in 1960, devised a plan in which northern college students would go to Mississippi in the summer of 1964 to assist in the registration of Black voters and in the operation of Freedom Schools for children in districts where public schools had been closed to avoid racial integration.

Recruitment at northern colleges generated numerous applications, of which McAdam was able to recover 959 forms and corresponding addresses for 556. Of these individuals, 382 had actually participated in Freedom Summer, and another 174 had been accepted as volunteers but for various reasons were unable to participate. In 1984–85, 20 years later, McAdam sent surveys to these adults and interviewed 40 of the volunteers and 40 of the no-shows. The applicants came from families of above average incomes, with "elite" colleges contributing 40% of the applicant pool. Forty-six percent of the applicants came from Illinois, New York, and California, fewer than 10% were Black, and the average age was 23.2 years.

In trying to recapture why students had volunteered, McAdam found that most were driven by an idealism that was informed "by a sense of generational potency" (46). As Keniston (1968) had found for war protestors, most volunteers were not rebelling against parents but "were acting in accord with values they had learned at home" (49). McAdam found that 62% had belonged to political, church, and other kinds of organizations (63). Using the original applications, McAdam also found that volunteers and no-shows did not differ in attitudes but that the latter group was younger and had more females.

The immediate impact of Freedom Summer was that 17,000 Blacks tried to register at courthouses, although only 1,600 applications were accepted, while 3,000 to 3,500 children attended schools. Impact was also measured on participants, who learned firsthand about southern rural poverty by living with Black families in their substandard houses. The idealism of volunteers was met with the harsh reality of the structure of segregation. Over the summer, participants witnessed 4 killings, 80 beatings, 1,000 arrests, and 67 bombings of churches, businesses, and homes.

Some events were heady and led to a sense of liberation and exhilaration, which was manifested in intense political discussion and experiences of sexual freedom. This radicalization formed roots of activism that soon sprung up on the nation's campuses and brought with it feelings of forging a new society, "something larger than themselves" (137). Indeed, one of the volunteers paraphrased Flacks's language when he recalled being "part of a . . . historic movement . . . you were making a kind of history" (138). This same volunteer also paraphrased Erikson when he said, "[Y]ou were . . . in some way utterly selfless and yet found yourself."

Several longer-range results were noted. Many of the volunteers subsequently became leaders in student organizations that led free speech and antiwar protests in the 1960s. Many of the female volunteers continued their political activities in women's movements (178), and both men and women pursued work in labor organization, civil rights, and community development (193–94). Twenty years later, this orientation remained identifiable as the volunteer alumni continued to devote their energies to work that changes society in contrast to the no-shows, who took up more conventional occupations. Hence, contrary to the image generated by the popular media that the 1960s activists became middle-class conformists, the majority of volunteers remain politically active, are liberal, and volunteer more today than the comparison group of no-shows. For example, of the 80 individuals who were interviewed, 46% of the volunteers versus 33% of the no-shows were presently active in at least one social movement, and 70% of the volunteers versus 50% of the no-shows belonged to a political organization.

The experience of Freedom Summer was central in shaping identities of volunteers. They came to perceive themselves as having agency to alter the course of history. They began to view themselves as being committed to improve social conditions for everyone. And they eventually saw themselves as helping to shape national political and moral directions. In McAdam's view, "What volunteers had discovered in Mississippi was nothing less than the political significance of the personal. Encoded in this discovery was an ideology and rhetoric of personal liberation that, when fused with . . . an emphasis on political change, were to give the Sixties their distinctive cast. Over time, changing oneself came to be seen as synonymous with changing society" (234).

Flacks (1988) describes the Black leadership of SNCC in complement to McAdam's characterization of the volunteer students. Flacks terms SNCC "a crucible of identity" in which "workers shared risk and camaraderie and a vision of the future" (133). Although SNCC had a brief organizational existence, its leaders went on to have political careers, some of which are still operative. Flacks attributes this lasting identity to membership in "groups of principled people [who learned that they] could intervene in history by taking direct, nonviolent action to confront obvious injustice" (135). Like McAdam, Flacks sees historical times as a stimulant that, when coupled with organizational energy, encourages youth to form their lives in a directive and activist manner.

A second study is summarized by Fendrich in his book *Ideal Citizens* (1993). The title refers to Black alumni of Florida A&M University who participated in public protests against racial segregation in Tallahassee, Florida, from the mid-1950s through 1963. He estimates that from 1960 through 1963 about 69% of the students from this traditionally Black school participated in sit-ins, boycotts, and other kinds of demonstrations. Data were gathered from these student activists and from a comparison group of nonprotestors who participated in student government.

In addition, Fendrich reports on data from activist and nonactivist White students who attended Florida State University in Tallahassee at the same time. In 1971–73, or ten years later, 186 Black and 95 White alumni from activist and nonactivist groups were surveyed. And in 1985–88, or 25 years later, 114 Black and 101 White alumni were surveyed. Results from the Black and White samples are reported separately.

Ten years after college, Black activists had become ideal democratic citizens. Compared with nonprotestors, activists had sought more advanced degrees (58% versus 45%), had higher incomes, and belonged to more civic organizations. The two groups did not differ in political attitudes or behavior, but both groups were politically active; for instance, within the past two years, 97% had voted, 60% took part in political campaigns, and 40% had participated in a public demonstration.

The findings from 25 years later showed that former Black activists and nonactivists were similarly *ideal citizens*. Sixty-three percent had obtained graduate degrees, and many held high-status occupations. Twenty percent were employed by government, and 46% were employed in the education sector. Eighty-two percent kept informed on politics, 49% belonged to a political party, 31% were active in political campaigns, and 93% voted regularly. Moreover, there was clear absence of cynicism or alienation, as no more than 19% expressed distrust of police, congressmen, or local officials. Black activists differed from nonactivists in being more militant about "Black issues" such as making African history part of school curricula and working peacefully to change race relations.

Fendrich attributed similarity in the civic involvement of activists and nonactivists 25 years later to the fact that both groups were part of a generation of college-educated Black adults that had risen educationally and economically, as a cohort. They were able to take advantage of equal-opportunity laws and new hiring policies to gain political and economic power. Hence, both groups gained from having been the first generation of Black college graduates to benefit from the enactment of civil rights law and new racial attitudes. However, it is important to note that the civic activities of Blacks who were activists in their youth were more focused on an agenda of political and social reform than were the activities of Blacks who were not activists in youth.

Results for White alumni are equally interesting. Both 10 and 25 years later, activists differed from the nonactivists. For instance, 83% of the activists, versus 60% of the nonactivists, had sought advanced education; 17% of the activists, versus 70% of the nonactivists, were employed in the private sector, while 62% of the activists, versus 17% of the nonactivists, were in education and helping professions. While alumni of both groups voted at a rate of 97–100%, the former activists were more likely to have recently participated in a protest march (62% versus 7%) and to have attended a protest meeting (75% versus 37%).

A Theoretical Framework

We propose that Erikson's position on identity provides a way to understand how service makes a long-term impact on youth participants. When youth are given opportunities to use their skills to redress social problems, they can experience themselves as having agency and as being responsible for society's well-being. When they participate as a cohort and when participation is encouraged by respected adults, youth begin to reflect on the political and moral ideologies used to understand society. It is this process of reflection, which takes place publicly with peers and adults, as well as privately, that allows youth to construct identities that are integrated with ideological stances and political-moral outlooks.

The data that support this framework come from actual lives of individuals in real historical time. They do not come from experimental results in controlled situations. Nevertheless, the clarity of the match between Erikson's ideas and the results suggests their usefulness for specifying the processes by which service makes its developmental impact. Gaining a sense of agency and feeling responsible for addressing society's problems are distinguishing elements that mark mature social identity. When identity is then integrated with a clear political or moral ideological stance, individuals are able to transcend the moment and draw meaning from society's history, which, in turn, makes it possible to face the future with hope and confidence.

This is the theory we used to frame the study of service that we report in subsequent chapters.

CHAPTER THREE

Community Service at St. Francis High School

Chapters 1 and 2 laid the theoretical groundwork for connecting Erikson's ideas on identity development with community service. We will now illustrate the theory's applicability with a case study we conducted during the 1993–94 school year. Our main goal was to investigate the *processes* through which service influences identity formation.

This case study was designed in response to two challenges articulated by reviewers of existing literature on the effects of service in youth (Conrad and Hedin 1982; Hamilton and Fenzel 1988; Newmann and Rutter 1983). One is to connect service experience to an appropriate theoretical understanding of social and personal development of adolescents. The other is to implement an appropriate methodology that illuminates process and is sensitive to influences of service.

In the present chapter, we introduce this case study by describing the service program, its participants, and the research procedures we used to assess the impact of service on the student participants. The study began in September 1993 and continued through the end of the academic year in May 1994. We gathered data throughout the year via questionnaires, quarterly essays, quarterly discussion groups, and observations of the students in class, at the service site, and on field trips.

It is notable that the students who form this case study were predominately Black and middle-class. Investigations of the service experiences of Black adolescents are needed because much of the empirical work in developmental psychology, particularly on prosocial behavior, has drawn from White samples (Hart et al. 1995). We also believe that Black urban adolescents attending a parochial school offer a particularly appropriate group for clearly illustrating the impact of service within a specific ideological and social-historical context. These points, however, should not confuse our argument that the theory that this case study exemplifies is a generalized one for adolescent identity development.

37

Community-Service Program

The school-based program we selected to study was founded in 1975 at St. Francis High School by the same teacher who organized it during 1993–94. The teacher, Mr. Siwek, had worked at a soup kitchen and wanted students, in his words, "to see poverty close up, . . . to sit down and share a meal with someone whose life is so totally different from [their] own, to have an opportunity to do something that is totally for others, to go home and think about what [they] have done; and then to share that experience with [their] family." During the school year, students were scheduled to work at least four times, for approximately 20 hours, at a soup kitchen located in the basement of a downtown church, only minutes from the nation's capitol. Students were encouraged to volunteer additional days over school holidays. During the school year, over 50% of the junior class went more than four times, with 7% going seven or more times.

St. Francis High School

St. Francis is a nonelite parochial school with a student population of approximately 600. It is located in an urban section of Washington, DC. The campus comprises a large brick building constructed in the 1950s and an adjacent football field. The neighborhood of the school has a reputation for a high crime rate.

"St. Francis" was selected as a pseudonym for the high school because St. Francis's life was discussed in the social justice class as an example of a person who made a dramatic conversion from a life of material pleasure to one of caring about the conditions of the poor and about social justice. The school is not sponsored by a particular religious order. The faculty had a handful of teachers from a few different religious orders, but mostly comprised laypeople. The faculty and staff of approximately 60 had a nearly equal distribution of Black and White men and women, with a few faculty from other ethnic backgrounds. The social justice course was taught by two laypeople, a White man and a White woman. During the year of data collection, the principal who was in charge of the day-to-day running of the school, was a Black laywoman, and the president, who raised funds and embodied the moral vision of the school, was a Black Jesuit priest.

Although the school is sponsored by the Catholic Church, the student population was 40% Catholic and the rest almost entirely other

Christian. The students' ethnic backgrounds were 95% Black, 1% White, and 4% other minorities. Parents represented a mixed socio-economic background that can be described generally as middle-class. Many parents were government employees. A few were lawyers, accountants, and doctors; a few had experiences with welfare and homelessness. Twenty percent of the students received some form of financial aid to help pay the annual tuition of $3,500 and for uniforms and books.

The school drew almost all of its students from urban neighborhoods in DC and Maryland with predominately Black residents. Few students lived in the affluent suburbs that surround DC.

Parents selected St. Francis for its academic reputation, discipline, athletic tradition, and Christian values. They valued education and set high goals for their children. School literature for prospective parents indicated that, between 1990 and 1994, 97% of graduates had gone on to higher education, and alumni had earned entrance to some of the most competitive institutions in the United States.

Social Justice Course

The social justice course was the third in a four-course sequence in religion, required of all students. The course met five days a week for 50 minutes; there were six sections of 20 to 30 students. Mr. Siwek taught five sections and Ms O'Connell taught one. All sections used the curriculum developed by Mr. Siwek and had nearly identical readings and assignments.

The goal for the course is well captured by one of Mr. Siwek's favorite assigned readings, a column by Jonathan Yardley. When Martin Luther King Jr.'s birthday became a national holiday, Yardley (1986, C2) wrote about his own college experiences advocating civil rights in a school newspaper: "It was my enormous good fortune to be at the right place in the right time: to be young, to have found a great cause, to be doing nothing of moment on its behalf, but to be doing it with all my heart." The teachers wanted to convince their students by the end of the course that they too were "at the right place in the right time," that they were young and could find a great cause to fight for with all their heart. To this end, both teachers used class time to implore their students to think about the moral implications of events going on around them and to care deeply about injustices. Issues covered in class in-

cluded homelessness, poverty among families and children, exploita-
tion of immigrant laborers, urban violence and capital punishment,
AIDS, racism, anti-Semitism, and homophobia. In addition, people
such as Martin Luther King Jr., Dorothy Day, Archbishop Oscar Ro-
mero, Cesar Chavez, and Mitch Snyder were offered as moral exemplars who devoted their lives to just causes.

The course text was a compilation of articles, many from the *Washington Post*, the *New York Times*, and the *New Yorker*. In addition to these
readings, the class viewed several films and public television programs,
heard guest speakers, and participated in special events such as reading their essays at the school food drive, seeing the musical *Les Miserables*, and visiting the Vietnam Memorial, Arlington Cemetery, and the
Holocaust Museum.

When students were asked about the connection between the social justice course and their previous religion courses, an almost unan-
imous response was "There is none." Most students described the
course as dealing with "reality" in a way that the Old and New Testament courses that were required during the freshman and sophomore
years had not. A few students noted connections between previous religion courses and this one in the following terms: the prior courses
reviewed what Jesus said; this course encouraged the students to live as
Jesus lived by serving the needs of the have-nots. In general, students
responded positively to the teachers' broadly encompassing approach
to religion. They appreciated Mr. Siwek's jokes about some of the stories in the Bible and adoption of the *Star Wars* trilogy metaphor about
using "the force" to fight "the dark side." In fact, Yoda, the *Star Wars*
character who instructs young Jedi knights in the way of "the force,"
was more frequently referred to in the class than God or Yahweh.

The course was framed in a clear ideology that combined liberal
politics with Christian activism. Government and corporate institutions were scrutinized for their role in perpetuating or redressing conditions of inequality. The students and famous people, such as athletes
and entertainers, were criticized for their failure to fight injustice in
any form. For example, when the class discussed what should happen
to a teenager who shot a four-year-old girl in a playground, the students were divided, offering answers ranging from "He should fry" to
"Only God can judge." Mr. Siwek made his stand clear in referring to a
character from a popular film that most students had seen. At the beginning of *Menace II Society*, a Black male teenager named O-Dog robs a

liquor store and brutally shoots the owner, and in subsequent scenes, he is shown killing other people in a coldly casual way. Of O-Dog and other youth offenders, Mr. Siwek said, "You made O-Dog what he is. It's your responsibility. Before he was a menace, he was a victim. Four-year-olds who get shot, five-year-olds who want to die, sixteen-year-olds who kill."

Franklin D. Roosevelt and twentieth-century Catholic theologians Pierre Teilhard de Chardin and Karl Rahner provided ideological influences that shaped the course's definition of moral action. Though Roosevelt was rarely mentioned in class by name, the teachers advocated his vision of the government's responsibility to act benevolently and provide a "safety net" for all citizens. Showing his own devotion to Roosevelt, Mr. Siwek once mentioned Roosevelt in class and with a smile proceeded to kneel and cross himself while genuflecting.

While Teilhard de Chardin and Rahner were not directly discussed in class, both Mr. Siwek and Ms O'Connell had studied their writings in graduate school and acknowledged their influence on the course philosophy. Both theologians addressed the role of Catholicism in "the modern world" and emphasized faith in practice, rather than in theory. Teilhard de Chardin's integration of scientific and Christian perspectives on evolution matched the course's focus on the students' role in the evolution of humanity (see Teilhard de Chardin [1955] 1975). Students were told to think about their actions in terms of whether they helped to move humanity forward or backward. For example, students were told that, whereas not caring about homelessness was "1993 behavior," caring about it represented behavior of the future.

Rahner's emphasis (1979) on the embodiment of faith through symbolic gestures of hope was found in the course's central message that even in the face of the most extreme hardship there is hope. In accordance with this view, the course stressed the power of individual gestures. The teachers encouraged students to surprise others by helping them. For example, Mr. Siwek told a student who had been insulted by someone about the food at the soup kitchen that he should have gone to McDonald's and bought the person a meal. For another example, at Christmas students were given the assignment of performing "random acts of kindness." These acts could be for a stranger, friend, or relative and did not necessarily have to take a great deal of time or cost money. Students were praised for doing something thoughtful and unexpected such as passing out homemade lasagna to homeless people on the street, painting the living room for one's mother, or filling parking meters that had run out.

Social Justice Teachers

While Mr. Siwek conducted his class in an energetic and unpredictable fashion, alternating between humor and anger, Ms O'Connell displayed a quiet and steady intensity. Both teachers had admirers and detractors among the students. Students described Mr. Siwek as entertaining, but they sometimes resented his opinionated manner. Students appreciated Ms O'Connell's dedication to social justice, but found her less entertaining than Mr. Siwek.

Before coming to St. Francis, Mr. Siwek served in Vietnam, studied at a seminary, and was fired from two schools. In his late 40s, Mr. Siwek was a highly visible teacher in the school, where he had taught for almost 20 years. During 1993–94, he played a very active role in fostering school spirit, organizing such activities as the Thanksgiving food drive and pep rallies for the athletic teams. He also supervised students who worked at school as part of a government youth program. One task that they performed was painting sections of the school, which they did creatively with pictures of the school mascot in the stairwell and words and quotes, including the name of the soup kitchen, along one hallway. Other gestures of commitment to the school included arranging tuition scholarships and organizing a weekend activities club for male juniors on school probation. While students were not aware of all of Mr. Siwek's actions, even his detractors thought that he was exceptional in caring genuinely about students and the school.

Students also seemed to appreciate the fact that Mr. Siwek's creative teaching style and intense commitment to the vision of his course sometimes got him into trouble with school administrators and other faculty. For example, some administrators and faculty felt that Mr. Siwek's course demanded too much time and attention and detracted from other important activities and course work. There was ongoing tension about letting students miss school and other classes in order to serve at the soup kitchen. In response, Mr. Siwek passionately advocated the pedagogical importance of his course. He was able to make the case convincingly that the course served as an integral part of the school's Catholic mission. In doing this, he secured the general support of the school's principal and president. It clearly helped his position as well that he was viewed by many alumni, students, and parents as almost a landmark of the school, having been there for almost 20 years.

The 1993–94 school year was Ms O'Connell's first. In her late 20s, she had previously worked among the destitute in Calcutta and had recently earned a master's degree in religion and culture. She came to the school with the goal of teaching social justice and was a staunch advocate of the curriculum Mr. Siwek developed. During the school year, her extracurricular activities included coaching a junior varsity girls' athletic team and starting a weekend activities club for sophomore girls on probation.

Serving at the Soup Kitchen

The service program used a time-release model. Each weekday, four to five juniors were scheduled to go to the soup kitchen from 8 A.M. to 12:30 P.M., in lieu of classes. At the kitchen, they prepared and served a meal for 300 to 400 people and cleaned up. Preparation typically entailed cleaning and chopping vegetables, making sandwiches and lemonade, and unstacking chairs in the dining room. Food was served from 9:30 to 11:30 out of two windows that connected the kitchen to the dining room. As people went through the line, students ladled soup into bowls and handed out salad, sandwiches, and fruit; some worked in the dining room pouring lemonade and busing tables. The tendency was to switch tasks so that students had an opportunity to do different things and because, while ladling soup was popular, one's arm could become sore and one's fingers burnt. In the final hour, students wiped down tables and counters, stacked chairs, cleaned the dishes, mopped the floors, and took out the garbage.

While preparing the meal, students tended to talk among themselves and sometimes with the supervisors. Occasionally, people who came for a meal arrived early and sat and talked in the kitchen. This did not occur frequently, as the church administration wanted people to stay outside until serving time. Typically, students had more opportunities for interactions with the homeless when they were serving and clearing food and on slow days, when they were sometimes encouraged to go into the dining room and talk to diners. On these occasions, many students played cards and talked with the people they met. One advantage of having all the students work at the same soup kitchen was that people who ate there regularly got to know the students and their school. Stickers bearing the name of the school's athletic teams were prominently displayed in the serving area, and students were often asked about the success of their athletic teams.

The majority of the diners at the kitchen were Black men in their 30s and 40s. Some had served in the military. Many looked physically ill. Drug abuse was a pervasive problem, and there were difficulties on several occasions during the year in trying to keep the dining room free of drugs and alcohol. It was relatively rare for families or women to come through the line, which may be accounted for by the soup kitchen's geographic location in the heart of the city. According to regular workers at the kitchen, the population served was becoming increasingly younger. They attributed this change to a decline in employment opportunities and low-income housing.

Two different groups supervised at the kitchen. On Mondays, a group of mostly elderly White women from an affluent Catholic parish in the suburbs organized the meal. The leaders of this group had served a meal funded by their parish every Monday for over 15 years. On Tuesdays through Fridays, a community of Black and White men and women who lived together and had ties to the Catholic Worker Movement provided the meal. Their food came from the Food and Drug Administration and from a local organization that obtained excess supplies from local restaurants and caterers. Some students expressed a preference for working with one group over the other. Students indicated that the "Monday group" served better food; some students also felt the Monday group was friendlier than the Tuesday-through-Friday group, while others voiced the opposite opinion. Mr. Siwek tried to schedule students so that they worked with both groups.

In addition to supervisors and classmates, students often encountered other volunteers working in the kitchen, particularly near the holidays. Students from other local schools and religiously affiliated youth groups from across the country showed up from time to time for a single visit. Additionally, one local school sent the same group of four students for two hours every Tuesday for half the school year. These students arrived in the middle of serving the meal and were usually assigned to clean dishes and prepare food for the following day. People completing court-mandated community service formed a final group with whom students worked. Typically, they talked little and were assigned more isolated jobs such as washing the dishes. Student interaction with other workers varied and depended partly on whether common work assignments were given.

Students

The entire 1993–94 junior class of 160 students participated in this study. Demographic information was collected at the beginning and end of the year. Table 3.1 shows that students were 48% female and 52% male, with the majority of students (67%) age 16 at the beginning of the year. The most frequently represented religious backgrounds of students were Catholic (33%) and Baptist (33%); 45% of the students attended religious services on a weekly basis, while 26% never attended. Students had high educational aspirations, with 54% planning to pursue graduate degrees. The last item in table 3.1 shows students' final course grade. While individual grade-point averages were not available, information on which students belonged to the honor society and which were experiencing academic difficulties suggests a correlation between the grade they received in this course and their overall average.

Individual information on socioeconomic background was not available, but there is no reason to believe this class differed from the school's general population. Information on home addresses indicated that many students came from neighborhoods marked by poverty, crime, and fear. To illustrate the living situations of students, we offer the following excerpts from an assignment in late October. Students were asked to write an essay expressing their perspective on violence.

"Every night where I live you hear gun shots, sirens, and screaming from children as well as adults. I get very mad when I sit down and think about what's going on. Why can't a child who is born in Washington grow up and live their life without the worry that they may get robbed, stabbed, shot, killed, or hurt?"

"I, as a person of only sixteen years of age, have been to too many funerals, cried too many tears over my friends' deaths, or serious injuries, and I'm tired of it."

"One of my friends was shot 10 times while I was in a store on M . . . Avenue . . . I feel there is nowhere to hide. I keep thinking to myself you could be next or someone I love could be next."

"I would like to start off by saying the violence is not inherited, it is taught . . . If your environment is violent, you will be violent because that is all you know, you don't know how to back away or let something ride. Calling somebody stupid in some sections of this city could cost you your life."

Table 3.1 Student Demographic Information ($N = 160$)

Variable	Category	Frequency
Sex	Female	76 (48%)
	Male	84 (52%)
Age (beginning of school year)	18	1 (1%)
	17	23 (14%)
	16	108 (67%)
	15	4 (3%)
	Missing	24 (15%)
Religious background	None	10 (6%)
	Catholic	53 (33%)
	Baptist	53 (33%)
	Other Christian	31 (20%)
	Muslim-Catholic	3 (2%)
	Missing	10 (6%)
Frequency of attendence at religious services	Never	41 (26%)
	Yearly	9 (6%)
	Monthly	27 (17%)
	Weekly	73 (45%)
	Missing	10 (6%)
Degree aspiration	High school only	2 (1%)
	Attend college	6 (4%)
	Bachelor degree	55 (35%)
	Master's/doctorate	87 (54%)
	Missing	10 (6%)
Course grade	A	60 (37%)
	B	33 (21%)
	C	48 (30%)
	D	18 (11%)
	F	1 (1%)

To gain a broader sense of the lives of these students, we gathered data on their participation in school and nonschool activities during the year. Notable findings are that 61% of students were involved in at least one school activity, with 40% belonging to an academic club or the yearbook and 39% participating in a team sport. Football and boys' and girls' basketball were particularly popular teams, with the football team having won its division championship several times. In terms of nonschool activities, 29% worked in part-time paying jobs, and 53% participated in youth groups outside of school.

Information was collected on students' prior community-service experience and on whether they had family and friends who participated in community service. Sixty-seven students (45%) had previously participated in service, and findings indicate that it was common for students to have family who participated (42%) as well as to have friends who did (25%).

Of the 67 students who indicated they had participated regularly in service, 75% did so five or more hours per week. Twenty-three percent said they became involved through a church organization, and 28% got involved through relatives or friends. Thirty-four percent of these students had done services for children, and 19% had done services for elderly adults. When asked to describe who sponsored the service activity, churches were named 42% of the time, and local community organizations were named 34% of the time.

Procedure

The teachers introduced the second author (MY) to the students at the beginning of the year. They explained that she was from Catholic University and would be collecting data for a research project on community service. Throughout the year, MY performed the role of teaching assistant for the social justice class and, in this role, ran discussion groups, substituted on three occasions, and co-led two field trips.

The students treated MY like a college student, rather than like a teacher. They called her by her first name and felt comfortable cursing and criticizing other teachers and the school administration in front of her. The comments of several students made it clear that they perceived her as younger than she was. They expressed surprise when they learned she was married. This perception was encouraged by MY's consciously nonprofessional dress. Working with students on physically arduous and messy tasks at the soup kitchen may have enhanced this perception. Students also felt comfortable referring to the fact that MY is White; on several occasions in discussion groups, they asked about her views on ethnic stereotypes and racism.

Data were collected from questionnaires, essays, discussion groups, and observations over the school year. These data were modifications of evaluative instruments and essays that Mr. Siwek had developed in 18 years of teaching the course. Modifications were made in consultation with the teachers and with consideration of the educational goals appropriate to this course.

Questionnaires were completed during the first week of class and at the time of the final exam. The questionnaires took 10–15 minutes to complete and asked about community service, religious background, and extracurricular activities.

Essays on the soup kitchen were written and collected after each quarterly visit. The first visit occurred between September and October 1993; the second between November 1993 and mid-January 1994; the third between mid-January and mid-March 1994; and the fourth between mid-March and May 1994. Students used a standard one-page form to write their essays. Directions on the top of the form read: "Write a thoughtful essay about your day of service at the kitchen. Comment on the work which you did and the people you met. Did you work hard, were you needed, did you leave some love behind?" On the bottom of the form, five lines were provided to describe the "best moment of the day." While most students limited their essay to one page, about one-third continued on the back.

We collected 436 essays of a potential 640. Forty-five essays were missing because students could not make their fourth scheduled visit to the kitchen. We found no background differences between students who handed in four essays and those who handed in fewer. In subsequent chapters, we report representative excerpts from the essays and refer to individual students by a number code that was assigned to them for the year.

MY also organized *discussion groups,* which were held after each class had completed its quarterly visit to the kitchen. Sessions were held during class hours. Groups comprised 10 to 15 students who met in a free room and sat in chairs around a rectangular conference table. After the first discussion session, students elected a leader to run each session. With the permission of the students, discussion groups were taped and later transcribed verbatim. Students were promised that individual comments would not be reported to teachers. The goal of these sessions was to give students an opportunity to share thoughts and feelings about their recent visit to the kitchen.

Over the year, 40 discussion groups were held. Again, we will report representative excerpts. Due to the quality of the recordings, we could not always match voices to particular students that we knew were in the group. We could, however, differentiate individual speakers. In reporting data, we refer to each group by its number code and to speakers according to the sequence in which they entered the ongoing discussion.

MY made *participant observations* at the soup kitchen on 11 occasions, approximately 44 hours, before the school year and 15 occasions, approximately 60 hours, during the school year. MY also attended 48 classes, observing from the back row. She attended special events such as the food-drive assembly, a pep rally, the field trip to *Les Miserables,* and the end-of-year assembly. After each observation, she wrote field notes.

We present this case as an ethnographic-like study that will help generate a model of how best to think of and capture service effects. We recognize the remarkable diversity of programs that the term *community service* covers. It includes everything from educational work such as tutoring, to environmental protection, to health care. The goal of presenting this case is to demonstrate a theoretical application that might be used by program designers, policy makers, and other researchers studying different kinds of programs.

Getting to Know Homelessness

In this and chapters 5–7, we present data that show the impact of the social justice service program on the St. Francis students. We begin with students' responses to the soup kitchen, homeless people, and homelessness. In subsequent chapters, we report how experiences with homelessness stimulated interest in related questions bearing on politics, morality, and Black identity. We start with the premise that minimum evidence of the program's effectiveness would be that students responded to homeless people and homelessness emotionally and cognitively. Such responses would indicate that service had an impact and was not treated merely as a requirement.

Nature of the Evidence

Students expressed their thoughts and questions in essays and discussions throughout the year. We report representative excerpts that are qualitative and signify what some or most students drew from their service experience. The rules we used for selecting excerpts were that they had to be representative of what several students wrote or said and they had to denote concepts unambiguously. Most of the essays were written in private at home on the day students worked at the kitchen, although we know some essays were written in study hall on the day they were due. Students were free to focus on any of the day's events or any idea these events might have stimulated. Given this frame, it is reasonable to view ideas that some students expressed as being potentially available to many students. Counting the number of students who expressed an idea would not adequately convey this point. But the fact that several students expressed an idea signifies its generality and potentially wider applicability.

We take a similar view toward ideas expressed during the dynamics of discussion. In a group consisting of ten or so students, particular ideas or arguments may have been discussed by two to five of the students. While only these students actively participated in the discussion of an issue, all students in the group were exposed to the several points of view that were expressed. Hence, mere counts of an idea or argument would not convey their potential impact on the group.

We first present data describing the preconceptions about homeless people with which students began their visits to the kitchen. We next show the immediate shift in perceptions students reported after making their first visit. We then report how students' perceptions became, on the one hand, more realistic and, on the other hand, more conceptually textured as they met and interacted with particular homeless individuals.

The second set of data deals with the broader ideas that serving the homeless provoked in students. It will be shown that for about one-half the students, service at the kitchen was an occasion for exploring homelessness as a social problem and provoked students to question their responsibility toward it. Service, of course, did not occur in a vacuum, as students were exposed to interpretations of homelessness by their parents, teachers, the media, the kitchen's organizers, and homeless individuals they met at the kitchen. Some of these views encouraged students to look at the conditions behind homelessness, and contradictions among the views challenged students to reflect on the validity of larger social claims. We show that, during the year, students developed their own points of view toward the causes of homelessness and possible responses to it.

We argue that this material exemplifies ways in which the service experience was implicated in the identity process. Insofar as students strove to understand homelessness, they were led to ask questions about society's responsibility for this problem, the need for government to solve it, its moral implications, and the relation of homelessness to other social problems, such as poverty. These ideas came from reflection on experiences at the kitchen and led logically to questions about students' own involvement in homelessness, such as whether they have responsibility to do something about it. This wedge into students' relationship to society may have opened them up to questions about other social problems and reflections on the kind of society in which they would like to live and the kind of political and moral values they want to prevail in that society. This questioning feeds directly into youth's quest for *transcendent meaning* with which the self can identify as it strives for historical rootedness and a stable future orientation. We illustrate this transcendent aspect briefly in the present chapter and elaborate on it in more detail in the next three chapters with regard to the self's relation to politics, morality, and Black identity.

Preconceptions about the Soup Kitchen and the Homeless

MY opened the first discussion session with each group by asking the students what, if anything, surprised them in their initial visit to the kitchen. Students in all groups responded alike and with vigor. They were appalled at the bad quality of the food they were given to prepare. They had not thought about the food they would be serving, but they were indelibly impressed with rotting vegetables and fruit, dry peanut butter, molding bread, and watery ice tea.

Second, students flooded MY with examples of ways in which the homeless people they saw failed to meet their expectations. Students expected them to be "dirty," "smelly," "mean spirited," "unapprecia-tive," "grumpy," and "disagreeable." While some of the diners satisfied these anticipations, others did not. Students discovered that most homeless diners were not smelly, repelling, or mean, but were mainly pleasant and appreciative of what the students were doing for them. Here we focus on expectations for the homeless rather than the food, because they give insight into the way that work at the kitchen altered students' views. All excerpts are from the first group meetings after stu-dents' initial visit to the kitchen.

In discussion group 1a, a female said, "I expected it to be lots dirt-ier, dirty people . . . And that's what most people think of the homeless—that they'd be dirty." A second female said, "I expected them to be all evil and grumpy, but they was nice. They chatted, asked you how you was doin', how your day was goin'."

In group 1b, a female said, "I thought it was going to be dirty," and a second female said, "They were really nice. I was expecting that they was going to be real pitiful and sad. Most of them were flirtatious, real flirtatious." Then a male student added, "I thought they were going to be mad at the world, you know. I mean some of the people down there—they was needy."

In group 3a, a female said, "I expected [the soup kitchen] to be much dirtier . . . but it was rather clean." A second female said, "I ex-pected the people to be hostile to me, but it wasn't like that."

In group 3b, a female said, "Well, I expected to see grumpy old people just running around—all drunk and all drinking wine and stuff. What I saw was, um, it was different."

In group 4b, a female said, "They were funnier than I thought. I mean, I didn't know they was going to have such a sense of humor." A male added, "Plus, I mean, most of the people in there was courteous to me. You know, 'Hi, how you doing?'" A second male said, "I thought there would be a whole bunch of old people just sitting around. And some drunks. But it wasn't that way. I thought it was going to be all stinky and dirty, pee spots and whatever. People were nice. There were still some crazy ones, but some of them were educated."

Each group invariably repeated their negative preconceptions, but then said that they discovered the homeless diners were, in fact, ordinary people in difficult straits. As one male stated it, "They seemed like everyday people. They just had problems."

We were able to verify students' negative expectations with another result. In some discussion groups and in 24% of the essays, students said that on their initial visit to the kitchen they were "scared" and "nervous," either expecting the worst or not knowing what to expect. For example, a female in group 1a said, "I was nervous 'cause I have never personally had a one-on-one conversation with a homeless person." And a female in group 7a said, "At first I was scared. I didn't know how people was going to react. I thought they was going to react toward us real mad. But they didn't."

Another example comes from student 502's first essay: "I arrived at [the soup kitchen] at exactly 8:00. I was very nervous about going there because I didn't know what to expect." In another instance, student 522 wrote in her first essay: "After mopping, sweeping, and stacking crates, it was time to feed the people. At this instant my heart dropped and I began to become scared. Why? I feared I wouldn't know what to say or how to act [as they came through the line]."

We show in chapter 6 that meeting homeless people was a case of confronting the *other*, someone who is so different from you that you are jarred into recognizing the difference and stirred to reflect on your own personhood as well as theirs. As many students said, the mere thought of meeting and having to talk to someone who was homeless made them anxious. For example, one female student (202) wrote: "This man stopped me to show a picture he had taken. I was scared of him because he was homosexual and I have never really talked to this kind before." We argue later that one reason this service experience made its intended impact was that it forced these 16-year-olds to meet and interact with people who were initially so different than they, that sufficient uneasiness was aroused to stimulate a healthy reflection on self, other, and their possible relationship.

Getting behind Homelessness: Looking for Causes

Usually by their second or third visit to the kitchen, students felt more at ease with the homeless and described them in realistic and particular terms. This seemed due to two factors. First, the kitchen typically served from 300 to 400 people per day. By ladling soup, observing, and interacting with these diners, the students had ample opportunity to differentiate the vague composite of "the homeless" into specifiable individuals and types. Students mentioned several ways in which the diners differed from one another. Some were old, and others were young. Some were drunk, and others were sober. Some were addicts, and others appeared to be "normal" people out of work. Some were polite and gracious, while others were rude and aggressive. Some were clean, but others smelled, making them difficult to be near or to look at. Some were not homeless but were among the working poor who came to the kitchen for a free meal in their security-guard or messenger uniforms. Still others were difficult to define because they came dressed in new clothes, had briefcases, or carried beepers. And still others were recognizable acquaintances—a neighbor on welfare or a distant relative who had recently lost his job.

A second means for differentiating among the homeless was through conversations in which the diners told biographical stories to the students. As stated above, opportunities for student-diner conversation typically came after food was served, and students were encouraged to go out from behind the counter to the dining area to clean tables and to interact with the people who were talking, playing cards, and resting. This usually did not occur until the second visit, and even then, many students expressed anxiety about leaving the security of the kitchen and interacting directly with the homeless diners.

In most of the reports, students said that the homeless initiated conversations with them. A typical story began when a homeless person thanked a student for coming to the kitchen to help. The person might then give a brief synopsis of his or her life and offer the student advice. For example, several homeless people told students that they had gone to college but either lost their job or became addicted to drugs or alcohol. They often mentioned a feeling of loss at being separated from their families. After describing themselves, they often offered students advice "to work hard in school" or "stay away from drugs." For example, student 513 recounted in his third essay what a homeless man had told him: "Keep it up and stay on the right side of the road because he told me it was rough on the other side. I can only imagine what the other side of the road is like."

Another example occurred in group 4a's fourth session, when a male said, "It was the first time that, like, I talked to the people. I talked to a man named John . . . He was telling me he had two sons. And he told me how he got hooked on drugs. He told me not to do the same thing." Another male then said, "I noticed that . . . they always try to give you advice, like this man—he came through the line. He said, 'All you kids are doing something good these days.' But he said, 'Whatever you do, I want you to say no to drugs and if you don't say no to drugs, you'll be right on the other side of this counter.' "

The homeless diners told stories about their military service in Vietnam, alienation from family members, losing jobs, dropping out of school, and the like. The storytellers usually took responsibility for their homelessness and used themselves as negative examples that students were told not to emulate. Hence, the emphasis on staying in school to complete their education and abstaining from drugs and alcohol. These personal morality tales made sufficient impact that students repeated them in essays and discussions as notable moments in their visits. These tales put a human face on the homeless, who became real individuals with biographies that accounted for their homelessness and, interestingly, gave them sensitivity that was expressed in terms of concern for students' welfare. Thus, instead of finding that the homeless were enveloped in their own misery, these simple stories showed that the homeless could be caring people who, despite their problems, were concerned about students' well-being.

Still, students were not blind to the bleak reality they saw at the kitchen. They witnessed knife fights that had to be quelled by the police. They were the objects of hostility, for example, being cursed at for ladling soup too slowly. They saw lewd behavior between pairs of diners and shared stories about being propositioned by homo- and heterosexual diners. They talked with diners who seemed to have lost their memory and were mentally enfeebled. The diners were of all ages from infancy through old age, and all ethnic varieties. It is understandable, then, that in four visits students would overcome any simplistic preconception they might have had.

It became increasingly difficult to fit all the diners into a unitary category of "the homeless" because students observed variations, got to know personal histories, and experienced expressions of goodwill from some of them. As student 618 wrote in his fourth essay, "I've realized that they are human beings and people's mothers, fathers, sisters, brothers, and someone's child."

While this study was in progress, homelessness was in the news on several occasions. For example, the television show *60 Minutes* did a report on abuses in a well-known DC shelter for the homeless whose director had previously come to the social justice class to talk with the students. The orientation of the report caused concern among the students, who felt the show producer's had purposely emphasized the negative side of what was, overall, a worthy project.

In addition, homelessness had figured rhetorically in the previous year's presidential campaign, via talk about housing for the poor and the widening income gap, supposedly resulting from 12 years of the "trickle-down" economic policy. Also during the winter, the local media reported a dramatic event of a homeless woman who froze to death one frigid night, alone, huddled on a bench across the street from the Department of Housing and Urban Development.

The teachers of the social justice class gave students numerous lectures on the relation between government policy and homelessness. Emphasis was put on the need for affordable housing, making job training and jobs available, and rearranging priorities in government spending away from defense toward reducing poverty and its effects. It is not surprising, therefore, that events at the kitchen led students to look further for causes of and society's responses to homelessness.

Throughout the year, students grappled with the question of who was responsible for homelessness—individuals who were homeless, government policy, anonymous economic forces, or citizens who passively watched homelessness spread in their communities. As best we can determine, students failed to reach consensus, but kept debating the matter throughout the year. We will now illustrate how students dealt with the issue of responsibility and, in the process of entertaining various answers, came to explore a rich range of alternatives.

A common hypothesis that students discussed was that homeless people were poor and homeless because they did not want to work.

One illustration of how students dealt with this assertion occurred in group 5b's third session. A female student asked the group, "I have a question. With all the stuff that's going on with homelessness, who is responsible? Do you think it's the persons who got themselves into it or society?" A male said, "Bill Clinton is responsible," and a second male said, "Society." A third male added, "I think it's more big business." The second male asked, "Big business?" and the third male said, "Yeah, check it out." A second female said, "All they gotta do is get a job." But the third male said, "I mean, the majority of what I hear of big homeless cases is because a large factory left a certain area and left a whole lot of people out of work."

Later during the same session, the topic returned to employment. The third male student above got impatient with those who thought homeless people ought to find work and said, "You go find a job. I'll bet you don't find a job in a week." But another male said, "I can get a job," which elicited the retort, "You can get a job because you got a house, you got an address." Yet another male chimed in, "If you [as a homeless person] wanna get a job, where they gonna call you? Where they gonna call to get in touch in with you?"

A similar discussion occurred in group 3b's second meeting. A male student asserted that "[the homeless] should get a job. Work." A second male said, "No listen, man. It's not that easy . . . it's not as easy as you think." A female said, "It's hard for people to get jobs. Even if they are trying to get jobs, they can't get jobs." The second male added, "Like my stepmother. I mean, she went to college and she, like, 8 years of college and she's an attorney and it's hard for her to find a job." But the first male said, "Brother, if you want a job, you want to work, you going to find work." The second male protested, "That's not always true. You see, you have better opportunities than [the homeless] do."

The issue of work and responsibility recurred throughout the discussions, and, not surprisingly, welfare was frequently brought into consideration. A typical instance occurred in group 4b's fourth session. A male said, "I don't think they should get rid of welfare because if you get rid of welfare, that would create a bigger problem. There will be more homeless. Welfare might be the only thing that's helping some people pay for their house or pay for food for their kids." A female added, "People, like, who can't work and they need it—but other people do and there [should be] some steps to build them up . . . so they become self-independent." A second female added, "When you're on welfare, it's like once you in, you trapped, because like, if you get a job, then you're cut off. They need better ways so you can get a job and yet, if it is not fully supporting you—" and a third female interrupted, "But they shouldn't just cut it all because of what she was saying, that they don't have any housing programs or educational programs where they can build themselves up."

These exchanges provide the kind of material that adolescents need to clarify their thinking about social complexities. Theories that emphasize construction claim that adolescents use private reflection to assess experience and make sense of events they witness. Individuals may correlate two previously independent ideas, reconcile an idea with new reality, or try to resolve contradictory thoughts. Indeed, reflection of this sort has classically been thought to be a hallmark of adolescence, since it allows construction of not yet seen but possible realities (Inhelder and Piaget 1958). If service can provoke such reflection, it directly nourishes the natural mental process that enables adolescents to make developmental advances.

The above illustrations show that, in exchanges during discussion sessions, students together did the mental work that theorists have attributed to individual reflective activity. Various students played alternating roles of asserting ideas, contradicting them, and trying to reach resolution. For example, the hypothesis that homeless people do not work because they are lazy was countered by the proposition that work is difficult to find, especially by people who lack skills and don't even have an address. This conversation was lifted to a higher level of causation as other students brought in factors such as government programs and industrial downsizing. The discussions did not end with clear conclusions that definitively eliminated alternatives. Rather, the participants teased out the pros and cons of various positions so that any conclusions an individual reached could have been honed by consideration of multiple perspectives.

The issue of responsibility for homelessness was given a well-rounded airing, which is precisely what some advocates of service learning have proposed ought to happen. They want students to begin thinking about society, how it is structured, and how it leads to phenomena such as homelessness. As we shall see in chapters 5 and 6, many students were not satisfied to stop with abstract reasoning but preferred to adopt plans for specific political action or to take particular moral stands. They were willing to make an individual choice that involved diagnosing the problem and assigning responsibility to themselves to be part of the solution. But for now, the aim is to show that work at the kitchen promoted the kind of reflective thinking that is beneficial to individuals' development.

Engagement

Another sign that working at the kitchen had an impact on students was the expression of emotional engagement. We noticed, in reading the essays, that students frequently interrupted their descriptions of the day's chronology with strong evaluative comments. We subsequently observed that similar evaluative comments often occurred in discussions, especially when the homeless had been depicted unsympathetically. We were able to score expressions of emotional engagement in the 395 essays reliably. This sample came from 119 students who handed in at least two essays, with one coming from early in the year and the other later. Three kinds of emotions were readily identifiable, *sadness, anger,* and *feeling good about helping.* Expressions of sadness occurred in 93 essays (24%) and appeared consistently throughout the year at the rate 21% to 26% at each assigned time. For example, student 401 wrote in her first essay: "I watched [an elderly woman] not only empty her soup into a jar, but we also watched her empty a bread tray into her bags. She was a small frail old woman with one tooth and a tendency to talk too much. But watching her look through the left overs and watching her save her food made me feel bad."

Student 302 wrote in his second essay: "The soup stayed plentiful but the salad ran out and [so did] the peanut butter sandwiches. I felt so sad because of what was being fed these people, stale bread, rotten potatoes and tomatoes and so on." And student 311 wrote in his third essay: "The worst moment came at the end of the day when John asked me to go wake up two guys and tell them to go. I hated having to do that putting them out of the nice warm building into the cold. After several hours of trying to help people feel better, it took 5 minutes to make me feel I made two men feel worse."

Students expressed anger about the inadequate living conditions and poor quality of services for the homeless at the kitchen. There were 38 (10%) essays with clear statements of anger, with 7% to 12% occurring at any time. In her second essay, student 522 wrote: "Something inside of me made me upset and angry when I thought about last time. The reason I felt this way was because people were not just hungry on Monday and deserved a good meal, but they are hungry all during the week." This student was making reference to the different groups that managed the kitchen, with the Monday group providing better food.

Student 509 wrote in his third essay: "As I stood there and stirred the peanut butter, I thought to myself, 'Damn they been serving these peanut butter sandwiches all year. Don't they know these people hate this shit.' I finally pinpointed what had been bugging me all morning. I was angry. In fact I was thoroughly disgusted. I was really pissed off about coming to the kitchen for an entire year and seeing absolutely nothing change." A third example comes from student 309, who in her fourth essay wrote: "This time I worked so hard. I wasn't happy. I was MAD. Not at the people there or the workers. I don't know who or why, I was just MAD. I began to think why doesn't the government give food [to the kitchen]. It ain't fair that they have to eat half rotten [food], half molded bread, and the same tired ass unchewable peanut butter."

Statements of satisfaction for helping also recurred across the year and were found in 99 essays (25%), although more frequently after the first visit (36%) than after the last visit (15%). In the main, students felt gratified when homeless individuals thanked them for helping, for example, "when a man came back and thanked me," and when "a lady said, 'Don't look so tired. I really appreciate [your] coming here and serving me today.' "

Three coders reviewed the essays, two for each essay. As a measure of reliability, Cohen's kappas were .73 for sadness, .77 for anger, and .69 for feeling satisfied with having helped. The coding was done without knowledge of the students' gender or the time of year when essays were written.

Transcendence

Our thesis is that, in constructing identity, adolescents look outside themselves for meaning that has historical stability and future promise. Adolescents seek to become part of places, institutions, ethnic groups, ideologies, and the like, which carry such meaning. In exploring them, adolescents give their emerging identities definable shape so that individual selves become part of identifiable collectives. Their actions thereby take on purpose and join the legacy of actions from previous generations, thus becoming individual representations of collective ideals.

Erikson argued that a lasting identity could not be constructed with reference to personal experience alone. The sole individual knows only anomie. Individual experiences are ephemeral, while identity partakes of relationships with other persons and society. By looking for transcendent meaning, adolescents seek to become part of larger historical entities ranging from families, to ethnic groups, to cultures, to humanity. Thus, by exploring the course's ideological stance toward social justice, students assessed themselves as actors within a tradition of helping the less fortunate in a spirit of mutual responsibility and respect. This ideology is deeply rooted in Western culture and is an articulated ideal of the various religious backgrounds of the St. Francis students.

Adolescents are not known for writing or speaking spontaneously in terms of history or abstract ideals. Fortunately, Luckmann (1991) has devised a definition of transcendence that offered a feasible approach for our purpose. Writing on contemporary religiousness, Luckmann proposed that transcendence need not be construed solely in its most abstract sense of finding unified meaning in metaphysical being. Instead, transcendence might be usefully parsed into levels ranging from *little* to *big* to even *bigger.*

An example of little transcendence involves recognition that one's own experience is the same as or similar to the experiences of another person. At this level, individuals learn that they are not unique but share experiences with others. At a higher level, transcendence exists in awareness that one's self-consciousness is shared by others who are similar cognitive, emotive, and spiritual beings. And at still higher levels, transcendence is defined in a sharing that goes beyond the immediate and experiential to conceptual participation in society or humanity. At all levels, transcendence involves recognition that aspects of one's life are shared with the lives of others so that meaning depends on the self's relationship with others, as individuals and as members of society.

The Present Application

How might service help students progress toward discovering transcendent meaning? Work at the soup kitchen exposed students to new and different experiences that stimulated them to reflect on their relationship to homeless people. At more abstract levels, homeless people

came to symbolize people who are different than the students, especially people who lived in less fortunate circumstances than they.
Homelessness also came to symbolize other problems related to poverty and the organization of society. Hence, in working with hungry
homeless diners, students had opportunities to reflect on all levels of
transcendence, from what they personally have in common with these
people, to the morality of letting them sleep on the streets in the capital of the wealthiest nation on the globe.

In a preliminary study (Yates and Youniss 1996a), we found that
Luckmann's scheme was useful for classifying statements made in essays. *Little* transcendence appeared in two forms. In one, students saw
through the stereotype of "the homeless" to acknowledge that homeless people are real human beings, differentiated individuals, and not
invisible figures whom you pass by on street corners. In the other type,
students perceived homeless people as ordinary humans living in unusual circumstances rather than unusual people in rare states. In one
form of *intermediate* transcendence, students encountered the fact that
they were taking their own lives for granted and became conscious of
such elemental things as having a warm bed, abundant food, and caring families who supported them in times of need. In a second intermediate form, students contrasted their good fortune with the
circumstances that led to or accompanied homelessness.

There were also two forms of *bigger* transcendence. In one, students reflected on the injustice of homelessness and the treatment of
homeless people by society. In the other form, students probed the
practical and political means for alleviating homelessness and their
own roles in solving the problems associated with it.

We applied this scheme to the present study, first by coding the
395 student essays. We found that 226 (57%) of the essays provided no
statements that were scorable for any transcendence level. In these essays, students described their day's experience at the kitchen in
matter-of-fact terms. The prototypical descriptive essay provided a detailed chronology of the day's events, starting with arrival at 8:00 A.M.,
moving to the first task of, for instance, cleaning vegetables, then the
next task of, for instance, handing out sandwiches, and so on, until the
diners left and the students mopped the dining area and went home.
But the remaining 169 essays (43%) contained statements clearly
representative of the transcendence levels. The same three raters
mentioned above read and scored the essays, with each scoring approximately two-thirds of the essays, using two forms of each of the

three transcendence levels. We obtained a Cohen kappa of .81, indicating a high degree of interrater reliability.

We also scored discussions for levels, but it was more difficult to get exact counts because of the fluidity of the exchanges. Nevertheless, we obtained a list of examples of each level by sampling the groups over the course of the year.

Little Transcendence

Form one was exemplified by student 601 in her first essay, when she described the stereotype with which she entered the program and noted how she came to see the homeless as human beings after she met them at the kitchen. "I kind of felt guilty because I thought of all the stereotypes of homeless people: dirty, smelly, mean, and grouchy people. Now I know a lot of them aren't. They're real human beings and here's proof."

Form two appeared in student 316's first essay. She noted that the homeless were like other human beings, but were living differently. "Although these people are homeless, I give them my utmost respect. I treat them just like I treat everyone else in my life. We should not put these people down for no reason at all. When I first saw them, I was scared. And I started to back out. But I said to myself that they are human beings just like we are. I don't see nothing wrong with these people. They live just like we do, but in a different way."

A mixture of forms one and two occurred during group 6a's first discussion when a female gave this reflection in response to other students' descriptions of how their expectations had been challenged on their initial visit to the kitchen: "I think this course has helped me in a lot of ways. Like I used to think the homeless—I didn't really look—I used to think bad of the homeless and stuff like that. I used to be scared of them and [thought] they were nasty. But then this course, you know, reading the articles, going to the kitchen, and writing things, comments, has really made me . . . look on a new level of how to look at the homeless . . . I never knew that they went through so many things."

Intermediate Transcendence

Form one was exemplified by student 201 in her second essay. She focused on the way serving the homeless provoked awareness of having taken her materially better-off life for granted. "On this one trip I also got to meet a variety of people I would never have seen if I were washing dishes or taking out garbage. Even after all my encounters with the homeless I still felt that these people are strange . . . It wasn't until one man who was passing through the line told me that the streets have messed up their heads. I thought about it and thought what would I be like if I was forced to live on the streets without knowing what the next day will bring. I go crazy when I don't have money for McDonalds. What would happen to me if I lived like they do?"

Form two was exemplified by student 529 in her first essay, when she expressed insight into the good fortune she had in contrast to the ill-fortune of the homeless people she met at the kitchen. "While I was [cutting up spoiled tomatoes] I looked at some of the rotting food and thought I would have thrown away most of the vegetables if I was at home. It's a shame that some of the food I waste looks better than some people eat. It was not at all as I had expected. Most of the people were smiling and playing and talking with friends. It was like a community center but I knew that some of these young and old faces I saw did not have a community, just a street corner. [A diner who was also a drug dealer] did not say anything I had not heard before but he made me think about how, as he said, we all could be just a step from not having a place to live."

Again, a mixture of forms one and two was found to occur in group 6b's third discussion. A male said, "For me the only thing about the soup kitchen is it lets you know if you don't see homeless people everyday—you get to see firsthand. I mean, you get to look at yourself and see how your life is and how you treat people. And like for me personally, sometimes I take simple things for granted—you know, 'Well, why can't I have this and that?' I know that's selfish of me, but I don't think of it. But certain things that I have, I mean, to a homeless person at the soup kitchen is like a luxury . . . To me, it's just regular and routine." Then a second male added, "I think from this class we need to start looking at what's going on in each individual life. Cause you don't know when the time might come you'll get sick and you can't pay for all your doctor bills and then they take your assets. You'd be out on the street and you're already sick. You never know when something like that might happen."

Bigger Transcendence

Form one was exemplified by student 106 in his first essay when he reflected on homelessness as society's problem and responsibility. "As

I handed out sandwiches and watched them eat hungrily, Phil Collins', 'Oh think twice, it's another day for you and me in paradise,' kept playing over and over in my head. It made me think, most of these people didn't seem to be afflicted by poverty, they seemed so like you and I. What really got [to] me was how young some looked—about 18 or 19. That's when I really realized that poverty has no bias and can strike at any time . . . the way society treats these people is wrong."

Form two was expressed by student 603 in her fourth essay when she reflected on using her own agency to correct the problem of homelessness. "As I looked around I saw so many faces; faces that were foreign to me and I was foreign to them. I wanted to see their souls, to know their stories, to be able to see what they see and know what they know for just one day. For I'm sure one day is all I could stand. There was a man there, I didn't catch his name, but he had an obvious mental problem, and my classmates and I laughed at his actions . . . Then I realized that he was going to be like that forever. There was no one there to help him, and probably no one who cared. It hurt to realize that I was sitting among society's forgotten. The people I read about everyday at school and in newspapers . . . They didn't need my pity. They needed my actions, and I didn't know what to do."

A mixture of forms one and two occurred in group 5b's third discussion as the students addressed responsibility to do something to change the status of homelessness. A female said, "Ain't nothing gonna change—drugs, guns, and homelessness. Ain't nothing gonna change until they recognize that people in high places are making money off other people's misery." A male then said, "I can't change nothing about the government. You gotta start at the top." But a second male responded, "Wait; here's another way. You can help by directing energy into being one of those people who are in top places."

Reflectivity over the Year

Our thesis is that service can stimulate reflective thinking about self-society relations, which feeds positively into the ongoing identity process. Recall that, of the 395 essays we scored, 169 (43%) contained reflective statements corresponding to transcendence levels. It seemed logical to ask whether some students started service already prone to take a reflective stance and whether service promoted reflection through repeated visits.

To answer these questions, we divided students into two categories, those whose first essay was descriptive and those whose first essay
contained reflective comments. In this assessment, we looked at only
the 98 students who had provided either three or four essays, because
only they could show cumulative effects of service. We looked first at
the 51 whose first essay was solely descriptive. Of these students, 43%
continued to be only descriptive in all their subsequent essays. These
students showed no signs in their essays that the program of service
made an impact on the transcendent dimension of the identity process. Of the remaining 57%, however, 41% gave a reflective comment
in one subsequent essay, 14% did so in two subsequent essays, and 2%
did so on all three remaining essays. Hence, over half the students who
started descriptively became reflective with further service at the
kitchen.

A different pattern was found for the 47 students who made reflective comments already in their first essay. Only 15% of them produced
subsequent essays that were solely descriptive and lacked reflective
content. Further, 36% of these students produced one more essay with
reflective commentary, another 36% produced two more such essays,
and 13% produced three more such essays. Thus, to answer our initial
question, not all the students entered the service program equally
open to reflectivity. Students who were already reflective in their first
essay were very likely (85%) to give reflective comments as they progressed through the program. In contrast, slightly over one-half
(57%) of the students who started in a descriptive mode became reflective subsequently.

To answer the second part of the question, students showed transcendent thinking proportionate to the point at which they started
the program. Those who began service with a reflective outlook retained that outlook throughout the year. However, it was also true
that continued service proved beneficial for students who started
with a nonreflective outlook, since 57% became reflective as the year
progressed.

Conclusion

This chapter has focused on how students responded to the soup
kitchen, homeless people, and homelessness. Going to the soup
kitchen as part of the social justice program encouraged students to
reflect on stereotypes of homelessness and to question its root causes.

Moreover, essays and discussions depict students' cognitive and emotional engagement in questions about homelessness. This engagement was expressed through intense emotional statements of sadness, anger, and satisfaction as well as evaluative statements that explored the transcendent meaning of the soup-kitchen experience.

CHAPTER FIVE

Forming a Political Habit

A major rationale for encouraging participation in service is to stimulate political thinking that will establish a basis for students' civic identity (Barber and Battistoni 1993; Boyte 1991; Flacks 1988). We showed in chapter 4 that many students used their experiences at the soup kitchen to reflect on homelessness as a phenomenon of societal structures and government policy. We will now present more details of the broader array of political thinking that work in the kitchen provoked. This report of students' thinking is organized around core ideas about civic identity. A democratic form of government assumes that citizens have agency to affect society through political processes. Agency, in turn, assumes that citizens feel responsible for supporting, correcting, and transforming social structures. A third idea that we consider is that, in a pluralistic society, intelligent citizens must be able to appreciate differing interests and know how to interact in order to persuade, hear out, and discuss differences so as to achieve mutual understanding.

Perhaps it is obvious that these are essential parts of mature political identity. We suspect that it may not be, however, because much of the literature on political socialization has been focused more on the formal content of government than on these kinds of political processes (Haste and Torney-Purta 1992). While knowledge of the number of U.S. senators or the rules for amending the Constitution are basic facts, they represent only a narrow piece of political citizenship. Leahy (1983), Lewko (1987), Flanagan and Gallay (1995), Miller (1992), and others have opened a new line of research into ways youth think about social issues and view the role of political processes in addressing them. This work informs our interest in civic identity, which includes development of a clear sense of political agency, awareness of how to be an effective person in a larger political community, and responsibility to keep that community functioning well.

For the remainder of this chapter, we review examples from essays and discussions that illustrate elements in the putative development of political identity. We realize there are no established criteria for defining the essential components of this domain. Our position, therefore, is that the cases reported should have clear face validity and fit reasonable theoretical stances, especially because we are studying identities in-the-making rather than already well-formed adult personalities.

Political Citizenship

Flacks (1988) has identified an important historical change in American youth's participation in the political process. Contemporary youth appear to have lost the capacity to perceive themselves as agents in the real political activity that continuously reconstitutes society. Flacks's contrasting point of reference is the span from 1930 to 1970 when youth took part in union organizing, served in World War II, worked for racial equality, and protested against or participated in our nation's military involvement in Vietnam, among other things. In his view, youth today provide a startling contrast in their seemingly passive stance toward the history being made around them. Perhaps society and culture seem too large to redirect or too complex to change. For whatever reason, youth in general seem to have reneged on their historic role as idealists who challenge tradition and seek a better society. Flacks's position may appear too radical for some tastes, but should not be discounted for that reason. Braungart (1980), taking a longer view of youth in the twentieth century, has reached a similar conclusion. Using Karl Mannheim's notion of generations, Braungart characterizes youth cohorts by decades and agrees that the post-1970 generation is notable for having opted out of the political arena. Boyte (1991, 765) carries this point a step farther by blaming the older generation of adults for having excluded youth from the political process, offering instead "senior-class trips to Washington, D.C., or exhortations to be 'good citizens'" as the stuff of civic education.

Boyte emphasizes civic responsibility by contrasting it with the proposal that service should help youth feel good about themselves (see also Kahne and Westheimer 1996). In Boyte's view, *being political* must go beyond the acquisition of a feel-good self-esteem and knowledge. It needs to lead youth to grasp their political agency and needs to generate a sense of responsibility for society. The experience of service should help individuals incorporate political orientations into the self, to an extent that politics becomes a "habit of the heart" (766).

We will now review excerpts from essays and discussions to show the degree to which St. Francis students manifested agency and responsibility. We describe students' consideration of the limits of individual initiatives, the role of government power and resources, and balance in the relationship between the individual and government. We then turn to the political issues students identified as important and assess students' understanding of their complexity and the associated entailment of normative political processes.

Agency and Responsibility

To what degree did students show signs that politics was becoming part of their habitual selves? Consider student 309, whose fourth essay described the kitchen's running out of bread and her having to go to a well-known shelter for emergency replacements. While there, she encountered a group of visitors who had come to see how a shelter operates. "There was a field trip going on while I was there. It funked my head. I mean, why would anyone want to take a trip to see how badly the world has treated people and how disfunctional the government is? How could anyone want to take a trip to see that unless they wanted to make things different? We already have enough people lookin and talkin with little action . . . It's my personal responsibility to change it."

Student 128 in her fourth essay expressed a similar dismay with talk and a preference for action. She happened to be at the kitchen on a day when some of the regular staff were going to rally at a government office to protest a housing bill before Congress. A few of the students were invited to participate in the protest by holding signs and passing out leaflets. Student 128, who went to the demonstration, wrote in her essay: "There is really *no* reason for anyone to be living on the streets anywhere. There is . . . a lot of talk about building more houses, but nothing is really being done. I know that there were not many of us there in protest and that we may not have really changed anything or made it better. I just look at it this way—we are a few of the group of people who were willing to take a stand. It was the first step of demanding better housing and I was part of it."

The notion of being actors in the political world was brought out also in discussion sessions. One interesting example occurred in group 4a's second discussion, which dealt with the behavior of homosexuals at the kitchen and a television exposé of abuses at a local shelter for the homeless. A female began by asking the question, "We're sitting here talking about issues, but what are we really doing? That's the question I have for all of you." A second female answered, "We are taking one step; we are discussing it. Discussing it, that's taking the first step." A third female joined in, "We ourselves, 16-, 17-year-olds, we don't necessarily have to do something right now because we don't have . . . power . . . If we get enough teenagers together, adults will listen to us but if it's like five of us, adults are not going to listen." The first female responded, "I'm not saying you go to an adult . . . I'm saying that it's just like that man sitting on the corner. It doesn't kill me to take a dollar out of my pocket and hand it to him. That doesn't kill me." The third female said, " I'm not saying that. . . ," to which the first replied, "I have power at 16. I'm sorry, I do!"

Limits on individual initiative. Agency introduces an obvious question about the effectiveness of individuals' actions in a large and complex society. Students raised this question by assessing the potential effects and limits of individual political action. One example occurred in group 4a's fourth discussion where racial segregation was mentioned with reference to poverty in Washington, DC. A female began with the optimistic statement, "We have the power to change [the world], but we don't do it . . . And if y'all sit here and say it's gonna end up bad—" A male student interrupted, "No one wants to step up!" A second female answered, "I am. I am. I am." The first female then responded, "You're only one person, but the world is real big." The second female retorted, "Martin Luther King—he came in and he changed something forever." A third female then said, "Well, I mean he changed segregation legally, but if you look out at the schools now, they're still kind of segregated."

A second example occurred in group 5b's first discussion. The group was discussing local politics and moving toward a negative outlook, which one of the male students tried to counteract by asking, "How do you know exactly who in the government is corrupt?" A second male student said summarily, "The whole government is corrupt." A third male asked, "What do you want to do, throw out the whole government?" A female student entered the conversation by saying, "Join Common Cause [nonprofit political reform organization]. You got to be committed if you want to change something. You can't say something is wrong and then just say, 'Oh, it's wrong, but there ain't nothing I can do about it.'" The second male then asked, "How did we get from homeless people to the whole government?" A second female inserted, "There's one thing I can't figure out. How to get the government to do something—something right, positive, good." A fourth male said, "To tell the truth, I think it's not going to take the government. Maybe it's going to take, I mean, people with a whole lot of money." A third female said, "I think it's the government. I think it's mostly the government." A fourth female then said, "The government's not going to do it. It's going to take good individuals just to change. I mean, you can't change the whole world. You can never do that. But you can change parts of it."

Spending public funds. The above statements show awareness of differences between individual and governmental action. This theme was developed further when students addressed the question brought up by a student in the preceding sequence: how can we get the government to do what we think is right? We note here that St. Francis students expected that government generally acts benevolently on people's behalf, although lapses occur when citizen intervention is needed. In group 4b's fourth discussion, this question played out as follows. A female started with the assertion, "It's the government's responsibility to take care of people here." A male picked this up by adding, "Instead of Somalia and all the other types of countries, they should keep the money here first." A second male said, "And you will hear people argue that forever. Like Defense first, number one!" A second female then said, "We have enough weapons." A third male said, "There's four or five buildings on 14th Street—destroyed during the riots. They can fix those buildings up and just make that a big shelter, like a hotel." The first male concluded, "All right, we have 28 B2s or whatever . . . those things are so expensive . . . You could dismantle one and take the money . . . You could do so much [with the] money. You could start the ball rolling."

The same topic was addressed by male 513, whom we cited in chapter 4. He wrote: "A guy who was sitting at the table eating . . . asked me if I was a volunteer . . . He told me to keep it up and stay on the right side of the road because he told me it was rough on the other side. I can only imagine what the other side of the road is like . . . Like the soup kitchen, the grates, the homeless shelters. I can't really imagine what it's like to be treated like an animal with no place to go. It's a shame to have a world with such poverty. All of this money that the government has and the first of it should go to the people. I wish I was in charge."

Another example was given by student 315 in his fourth essay. After giving a man in line an extra sandwich, he noted the man nearly "burst in joy. It was like he gave up asking people for things, in his mind everybody was selfish. I get so sick and tired of the government sending observers and satellites in space without putting some of those millions of dollars into [the] War against Poverty."

Government and responsibility. On confronting homelessness face to face, many students reflected on finding fault or responsibility, which led to reflections on government spending, wealth, and individual initiative. Two groups in particular drew out this theme by considering the several alternative causes of poverty and homelessness. In their first discussion session, group 5b happened on this theme when a male said, "I don't see how some people can be rich like that when other people who have absolutely nothing are laying out in the streets . . . I mean, talking about America and the American dream. The American dream is that everybody gets a piece of the pie." A second male said, "Yeah, but everybody should do that for themselves." The first male responded, "I think this country should be more a socialism government sort of thing—" The second male interrupted, "You're thinking of communism—" The first continued, "Because there's such a pole between the rich and the poor now . . . I mean, you can get out of [being poor], but . . . it takes a very strong person. And, of course, people need help . . . If you have resources to help someone like that, you should try to do everything you can do." A third male said, "I disagree . . . If everybody's got to get a piece of the pie, that makes it seem like, that you wouldn't have to work tonight. You'd wait for a person to give me a piece of the pie." A fourth male added, "You're right." But a fifth said, "There's a difference between being helped and not being helped." A sixth male said, "You can't help those who won't help themselves." This led to a discussion of minimum wages, caps on income, and the gap between rich and poor people.

A version of this same problem appeared in student 604's fourth essay: "I learned that there are still many questions unanswered, unfinished. In the United States there are about 7 to 9 million homeless. This is ridiculous. I know that I am still young and unaware to see the many other problems of the world. But I know that there shouldn't be homelessness and there shouldn't be poverty. Something should be done. Everyone needs to help one another."

Specific Issues and the Political Process

Frequently, experiences at the kitchen prompted St. Francis students to reflect on and discuss political matters that went well beyond homelessness but were pertinent to their milieu. These topics included improvement of schools, desegregating neighborhoods, laws to stop redlining in bank loans, responding to the spread of AIDS, building prisons rather than schools, using prisons to educate inmates, whether to legalize drugs, corruption of government officials who monitor the drug trade, removing cheaters from the welfare roles, eliminating welfare payments for children, programs to stop teenage violence, job training, corporations' responsibility for the health of local communities, and government officials' lack of empathy for people with problems, to wit, the homeless.

These concerns were pertinent to the environment in which the St. Francis students lived. These topics were familiar because of experiences of family members and neighbors, for example, a sister who cheated on welfare, a brother who was in prison, a neighbor who could not find a job, or a friend who dropped out of school to sell drugs. Not surprisingly, students often connected several topics in a single session. We briefly describe specific topics students brought up and then focus on discussions that allowed us to see how ideas were exchanged and re-formed through peer interaction. While agency and responsibility are essential to political identity, it is equally important that students get engaged in topics that bear directly on their lives and the lives of people they know. Only when political processes affect outcomes will they become more than textbook notions and be integrated into personal identity.

Prisons. We did not expect the topic of prisons to be related to the soup-kitchen experience. Crime and punishment for crime came up under several guises when students discussed, for example, stories about prison or drug use told to them by homeless people they met at the kitchen. A common lead was when a homeless person told a student "not to use drugs and to work hard at school" in order not to "end up on the wrong side of the road." The students were also aware of the often-cited statistic that more Black males between 18 and 24 are in jail than in school. On seeing young Black men, who were formerly in prison, at the kitchen, students remarked, "That could be me a few years from now." Hence, prison was a relevant topic to the St. Francis students even though as a group they were more likely to be enrolled in college than incarcerated, a few years hence.

The topic of prison came up in group 3b's fourth session when a student noted that he had seen a group of former inmates playing cards and hanging out at the kitchen. A female said, "People don't think it's anything to go to jail anymore. It's like, 'I got somewhere to sleep, I got somewhere to eat.'" A male added, "It's like a vacation," and a second female said, "I got another one. This man went to jail for bank robbery or something. Then he did it again just so he could go back and get a bachelor's degree." Others embellished this idea until a second male interrupted by saying, "My brother did that." The previous female contributor said, "We can't hardly afford jail," but the second male said, "My brother got his bachelor's degree in jail. I'm saying, what's wrong with that?" After some discussion, a new female said, "Okay, if you don't know they can teach you a trade, or get your GED, or something—but no degree and all that." However, the second male held fast by asking, "Why not? You need something to come out with . . . You['re] already one step behind everybody else cause you got a prison record. How you gonna get a job? You already got a prison record. How else you gonna better yourself?"

A different slant on prisons was taken in group 4b's fourth session when mention of crime led to discussion of a pending bill before Congress to build more prisons and punish crimes with harsher sentences. Some students favored this approach for handling rising crime rates, while others favored using money for prevention by building better schools. An extensive exchange followed and ended when a male student offered the following conclusion: "How much does it cost to lock one person up in Lorton [a local prison] for like a year? Like a hundred thousand dollars? I mean give me a hundred thousand dollars between the ages of 3 and 18, or whatever, when my fate is gonna be decided, and I'll guarantee you I'm not going to Lorton. You know what I'm saying? You know it pays off in the end."

Jobs. The matter of employment came up numerous times, as many students believed that homeless people ought to work rather than rely on homeless shelters and soup kitchens for survival. Other students countered these views by pointing out the difficulty of finding jobs, especially for people with personal problems and lacking job skills. And as one student above noted, when employers move out of town, communities suffer because workers have fewer alternatives for employment.

Group 6a's first session provided an example of students' considering several sides of the job question. This occurred during a discussion when a female student described a situation involving her sister who is on welfare. "I know a couple of people who abuse welfare; have been on welfare since '79. They keep having children so they can stay on welfare . . . My sister did . . . [When she was told her payments would end] she had another child. And now one of her children is 14 and the other is 3 months . . . That's just abusing it. I think after a certain number of years, if you are able and are still young, you [should] get a job." A male agreed, "Hell, yeah!" Another female agreed by saying, "They should make you get a job." However, a third female said, "But jobs are scarce."

Another orientation to jobs was evident in group 4a's fourth discussion about welfare. In the midst of the discussion, MY asked, "Do you favor abolishing or keeping welfare?" Several students favored keeping it. One of the females said that crime would increase if welfare were abandoned because people needed money to live. A male added, "They should do like they do in Maryland. When somebody got more than two kids, they make them get a job or they help them find a job." The female responded, "Yeah, I think if they do abolish welfare, they should help the people get a job."

Welfare. In the main, students were skeptical about the deservingness of people on welfare. As group 6a's excerpt cited above illustrates, such views were frequently supported with stories about welfare abuse. Another representative discussion occurred in group 1a's first session. A female noted that some diners were not homeless but were on welfare and came to the kitchen for free meals. She said, "I know a lot of people on welfare who don't need to be on welfare. They are capable of getting a job and they don't . . . I think the government should do something about it; they should make people work and give them a time limit as to how long they can be on welfare." A second female responded, "You can't really give people a time limit to be on welfare. There's no telling how they [got there] and why they're not getting a job. Some companies might not give [them] a job just because they are on welfare." The first female then said, "Well, just to say something about that, there's this girl in my neighborhood and she's 16 and she has a daughter and she's on welfare . . . She's in school but she could get an afternoon job." The second female, however, countered, by saying, "But if she's 16 and has a child and in school, don't you think it's kind of hard to work after school? She has a baby to take care of and homework and tests to study for." A third female added, "But she still has that responsibility on herself today. It's nobody else's fault." But the second female held to her view: "We all make mistakes; nobody's perfect."

However, a contrary opinion was expressed in group 3a's second session when, again, welfare reform was being discussed. A female student said, "Government has to play a major role in it, but seeing how the government's not, somebody's got to solve it." A second female said, "Because the people I encountered at the kitchen, the majority weren't homeless, but they were on welfare . . . The money that government gives . . . is not enough for people to live from day to day." The first female then responded, "It makes me so mad, when and if you're on welfare and the government's helping you, you're not allowed to save money. I mean, it makes no sense. They want people to get off welfare. But the only way to get off welfare is to have money."

Legalizing drugs. The topic of drugs entered discussions through several avenues, for example, meeting self-proclaimed addicts at the kitchen or noting the extent of teenage violence associated with drugs in Washington. A typical instance occurred in group 6a's second session when that day's elected female moderator said, "Let's talk about legalizing drugs . . . I just think we should legalize drugs because I feel like that would take all the money out of it. Ergo, it would take away the killing and most of the violence . . . Then that way, it could be regulated by government and that would bring in money to the government." A male responded, "But more problems would be raised." A second female said, "I don't think it should be legalized. You think it's going take away problems?" The first female responded to her, "Hold on, let me ask you something. Do you think anybody who really wants drugs is being stopped, just because it's illegal?" The second female retorted, "Do you think that would take away the killing?" The first female said, "It would help take away the majority of it because it's going to take the money out of drugs. Ain't nobody going to be on the streets selling it because the government's going to sell it." But the male student objected, "Crime rates will raise . . . if they can't sell drugs, what's going to happen? More crime's going to happen. Ergo, murders are still going to happen."

The same kind of discussion and conclusion occurred in group 5a's third session. One male said, "If you legalize drugs, less people get shot." But a second male said, "I think it's bad." A third male said, "I'm saying, if you legalize it, there's gonna be something else somebody's gonna be fighting over." And the first male said, "But still, you got to take away the major problem."

Politics as Habit

Our general thesis is that service within the context of a clear ideological framework can nurture adolescents' emerging identities in the manner proposed by Erikson. The point is not to teach an ideology for life, but to engage adolescents in reasoning they can extend, reject, or amend as they develop. The goal of the present chapter is to provide illustrations of early steps in this process. Students' personal essays and public discussions showed, first, that service promoted two basic elements required of democratic citizenship—a sense of agency and responsibility. Students began to analyze situations from a political perspective and to assess responsibility while estimating their own agency. In asking whether individual actions could make a difference in a problem so large as homelessness, some students believed that individuals could be effective, but with the qualification that they would have to work collectively or that individuals could be effective on a local level. Students also asked whether individuals could make a difference without the cooperation of government, which had the power and resources either to help or to impede reform. Some students seemed to be cowed by the prospect of confronting the government behemoth, wondering how individuals could move government to do what was right. Other students, citing the example of Martin Luther King Jr., responded that commitment was the key to get government to change, and still others had the insight that they themselves could become government officials in the future.

Responsibility cannot be treated wholly apart from agency. There would be little point to feeling responsible to eliminate homelessness or to better conditions for homeless persons unless one had the interest and power to do so. Students addressed these issues by showing interest in improving society and focusing on their power to "make a difference" in the immediate environment, for instance, in helping people at the soup kitchen smile, get a hearty meal, and find relief from the tough life on the streets. This may be a version of the adage that "all politics are local" in that political responsibility can be experienced most fully in face-to-face contacts. But students further realized that helping the homeless was everyone's responsibility and that the government comprises various citizen forces, rather than being an abstract thing apart from the citizenry. This shows the two sides of responsibility, a sense of communal belonging and using agency to better it.

Agency and responsibility gain a semblance of generality in the fact that students not only applied them to themselves but to the people about whom they were thinking. For example, in discussing prisoners, students recognized that, in order to have a chance at getting productive jobs, prisoners would have to be educated. In an interesting variation on this theme, those students who argued that homeless people ought to find jobs to become self-sufficient were countered by other students who pointed out that homeless people typically lack the skills that allow them to obtain such jobs. In still another variation, several students argued against current welfare practices by citing cases in which relatives and acquaintances abused the system. A fourth variation occurred with regard to the legalization of drugs when some students argued that their peers who sold drugs for a living would, after legalization, have to find alternatives for obtaining money.

A further sign of generality was that agency and responsibility were treated realistically and ideally in essays and discussions. In focusing on the penal system, welfare, poverty, and drug legalization, with respect to particular individuals the students knew, they reduced government from an abstract realm to concrete instances involving real people in situations they could immediately grasp. In discussing a brother who earned a degree in jail or a sister who abused welfare, students made political issues accessible and palpable.

We note that students took three approaches that gave the concepts some possibility of becoming part of their habitual political outlooks. First, some students recognized that the debating of political questions was itself a form of political action. It was called a "first step," implying that public reflection on issues was prerequisite to any form of political action. Second, some students argued that working at the kitchen, however small an act this was, constituted a productive political response to homelessness. Some students also magnified their actions to an imagined scale where the collaboration of many people would have a decisive impact on homelessness. And third, many students projected themselves into the future, when they viewed themselves as having more power to affect social change. These students imagined that as adults they would have money, power, or government positions that would allow them to address homelessness and other social problems.

Taking Differing Interests into Account

In individual essays and group discussions, students showed recognition of the dynamics that lie at the heart of government and politics. In our pluralistic society, there are diverse interests, each of which has a right to be heard. Expressing one's views, listening to the views of others, and seeking ways to reconcile views and understand one another are essential elements of our political process (Collins 1979; Gamson 1992). Consider the topic of lenient treatment of criminals. Surely, these urban students were not naive about crime and violence and had a well-based antipathy toward criminal behavior and the havoc it wreaked in their neighborhoods. At the same time, these students were conscious of the difficulties of the local job market, especially for people who did not follow the normative pattern of staying in school at least through high school graduation. These students did not excuse criminal behavior, but endorsed education and job training that would give criminals a chance at normal employment.

These kinds of interests are precisely what one finds in actual politics, for example, in the sides political parties took in the Omnibus Crime Bill and welfare reform, which were being debated during the 1993–94 school year. It is clear that the St. Francis juniors represented the several sides of these arguments and cannot be characterized as holding a monolithic position. Given the diverse views within this junior class, it is worth noting that the forms of argument we observed encouraged exchange of ideas and allowed opposing interests to be expressed and heard out.

We do not want to exaggerate the importance of these dynamics but stress how valuable they can be for emerging identities. The intensity with which discussions were conducted allows us to infer that these students were beginning to explore political positions with some seriousness. This exploration is basic to the identity process at this time, versus the alternatives of political disinterest or precipitous fore-closure. At a time when students are thinking out political positions, opportunities to express views and hear them reflected through the different views articulated by peers provide an ideal condition for ad-vancing development.

Civic Identity

The final point of this chapter pertains directly to Boyte's (1991) and others' proposal regarding the role of service in civic identity. Recall Boyte's tongue-in-cheek contrast between service that is demanding and field trips or lectures on citizenship. Boyte is critical even of ser-vice whose goal is a soothing balm of self-satisfaction. He calls this an "alternative to politics" (766) and seeks to replace it with service that engages youth in public affairs and politics that struggles with the problems that need to be addressed. Task solving is essential to any "generation [that] defines itself politically" (767).

In chapter 8, we review evidence that these signs of political agency in high school juniors have lasted in St. Francis alumni. For the present, we look at statements made by juniors as they looked toward their own political future. Student 405 on his third visit to the kitchen said he had talked with the kitchen staff who taught him a lot about the state of homelessness in the city: "They really made me feel a sense of urgency within myself. I now feel like I should join the Peace Corps or something. I will be a force in this world."

Other students had different experiences that provoked a similar conclusion. We refer again to the episode described earlier, when five St. Francis students volunteered to attend a demonstration at the De-partment of Housing and Urban Development. Three of the students described the rally in their essays, but gave no reflective comments. The two other students did, however. Student 128 said: "This day was very interesting and it leaves me to wonder, will I ever be one of those people who will be willing to take a moral stand? Will I continue to fight for what is right? Hopefully, I will. After all, someone has to do it. Why not me?"

Student 129 wrote: "In actuality our presence there wasn't such a big thing. A few people asked questions which we were prepared for. Other than that we just held up a sign and a banner, handed out infor-mation, . . . I have been to one other such thing which was a march for women's . . . choice in abortion a year or two ago, but this was a little different. I felt as if I was taking a moral stand. I am glad I got a chance to participate. Maybe I am a future activist . . . There were but eight of us . . . even though we may not have done much, we may have come one step closer, which is a lot better than standing still."

These excerpts illustrate the form of political self-consciousness that Boyte and others want service to stimulate. They want youth to become engaged in seeing problems as opportunities for political action, not distant events in Congress, but action that interested citizens can take. The goal of this action is to better society, especially for people who, for whatever reasons, are in less fortunate positions and can benefit from youth's help.

Conclusion

Service at the kitchen was no magic intervention that turned bored or cynical teenagers into instant activists. For some St. Francis students, however, service within the context of the social justice course triggered political awareness and steered the identity process in a useful direction toward political involvement. Students experienced a sense of their own agency either in the consequences of their actions or in being able to debate their ideas about a better society. Students also gained a sense of responsibility so that problems such as homelessness became issues of importance for them. Homelessness was a problem to solve not just for government, but for everyone in the community.

We emphasize that these students are high school juniors with much more experience before them on their way to adult citizenship. As we shall see with alumni, even the next step to college is fraught with challenges and difficulties. Nevertheless, we saw in this chapter that for many students the seeds of political identity were being formed as they pictured themselves as members of the community for whom political action was normal and right. This is as close as we can come to seeing the developmental process through which politics is shaped into a personal habit and being political is made an essential part of the individual's identity.

CHAPTER SIX

A Moral Gyroscope

While the most active portion of adolescents' political life lies in the future and is, therefore, virtual, the moral domain is immediate and concrete. The literature on service has emphasized the potential for civic involvement, but its role in moral development is equally potent. The aim of the present chapter is to show how the St. Francis program affected the moral component of students' emerging identities. We illustrate this general point by looking at the specific aspects of moral agency and responsibility, moral compassion, and the coupling of compassion with principles of justice.

As we showed in chapters 4 and 5, work at the kitchen was a springboard to explore the broader significance of homelessness. Of present interest, reflections were driven in part by the social justice curriculum, which persistently focused on the moral implications of homelessness. The teachers encouraged students to think about the irony of pervasive homelessness in the capital of the richest nation in the world. The teachers prodded students to analyze everyday reality from a religious-moral perspective and demonstrated the point by casting local events in political-moral terms. Service was designed to put students in contact with homeless people who differed from them and whose condition aroused questions about the distribution of wealth and government and individual responsibility. These issues were framed in a Christian theology of justice in which service to "the least" of persons was a fundamental moral command for everyone. Students were told to imagine themselves carrying on this tradition of acting in the cause of justice; hence, moral identity could become personal as well as collective.

We assume that the teaching of morality presents adolescents with options in their search for ideological clarity. While formal instruction can sensitize students to the moral dimension of everyday events, it is ultimately up to the students to construct meaningful moral stances. Morality is more than the memorization of precepts and prohibitions. It involves defining events in moral terms and acting to promote justice. Moral identity, then, unifies the self's basic orientation to society by combining cognitive, emotional, and behavioral elements (Walker 1995).

Students were responsive to the curriculum, readily recognizing its aims and distinguishing it from the previous didactic religion courses they had taken. For example, when MY asked group 4b in the first meeting how this course was related to their previous religion courses, several students yelled, "No comparison." One student said, "In religion, we read about the Bible every day; and still I don't know anything about what God did. But now I know how . . . to help the homeless . . . How to help . . . the have-nots." Another student said that this course taught students "how to apply Jesus Christ to your community." And still another student said he learned that "the church should not just be a place of worship. It should be a place where you contact the community. That's the most important thing."

Statements such as these indicate that the course's message was heard and was translated into students' own words. Emphasis was on the need to help others, to take responsibility for improving the community, and to work for justice. In understanding these charges as part of a religious-moral tradition, students were encouraged to become participants in a historically tested, transcendent legacy. Students were urged to assess this possibility so that they could determine whether they were persons who go out of their way to help others or whether this was too demanding for them to accept.

The aim of this course is compatible with an evolving theoretical approach that views morality as part of the person's makeup, rather than as judgment or behavior. Blasi (1984) has argued that moral judgment, for instance, was for too long considered a mental operation, a calculus, apart from persons' understanding of themselves as moral beings (see also Blasi 1995; Davidson and Youniss 1991; Hogan and Emler 1995). As persons assimilate moral reasoning and behavior into their self-definition, morality becomes integral to their identity. They therefore act morally as a matter of who they are and not because of an autonomous logical judgment, which, if anything, follows from identity.

For the remainder of this chapter, we focus on ways in which this program stimulated moral sensitivity by illustrating steps in the developmental process that theoretically leads to integration of morality with identity. We propose that this long-term process begins in simple acts of peeling potatoes or handing a sandwich to a stranger with a smile, and eventually gives rise to questioning the causes of homelessness and the relative roles of individuals, business, institutional religion, and government in attending to the needs of everyone in society.

Moral Precepts in Action

Experiences at the soup kitchen led to reflections on the moral aspects of homelessness, with the search for transcendence being based in elemental acts such as giving and being tolerant.

Acts of Giving

In expressing their reflections on the service experience, several students focused on charity in the form of giving to others in need. These reflections seem self-evidently part of a nascent moral system of thinking that is foretold in young children's definition of kindness as giving to others in need (Youniss 1980). Importantly, giving is something the St. Francis students have experienced and can do.

One question that recurred across discussion groups was whether one should give money to homeless people when they are likely to use the money to buy drugs or alcohol. As was shown in chapter 4, many students began service with the stereotype that homelessness is often due to drug and alcohol abuse. This expectation was reinforced at the kitchen, as students sometimes witnessed homeless people in stupors and manic states of aggressiveness that came from drug use. Additionally, several homeless individuals told students stories about their involvement with drug or alcohol addiction, which invariably included the didactic admonishment "Don't use drugs." Knowing that money given to a homeless person might be used for drugs or alcohol, students faced the dilemma that charity might unintentionally contribute to self-abuse. However, if students did not give money, the homeless person might be deprived of a meal, warm clothes, or a clean bed. Students expressed several solutions to this dilemma.

In session 1, group 1b discussed the proposition that one should give even when the money was likely to perpetuate self-abuse. A female said, "When you see somebody in need, and you have something that you can give them, you shouldn't just stand there. You should give them something." A second female asked, "Why give [money] to them . . . if they buy liquor and drugs?" A third female said, "I think, I mean, if they need [drugs and alcohol] bad enough . . . I hope it does them some good. 'Cause I mean, that's their business . . . And I'd give it to them and what they do with it, that's on them." A male student then said, "I mean, it's up to that individual. You can't rehabilitate a person if they don't want to be rehabilitated . . . They're going to make that decision."

A variation on this theme was produced by group 3b in its second session, which took place the day before Thanksgiving. The students contrasted their anticipation of tomorrow's family holiday with the bleak tomorrow homeless people faced. When one of the students was especially sympathetic to their plight, another student disagreed by saying, "Ain't nobody telling them to be no drunk, no drug addict." The first female said, "Sometimes they don't have a choice." But a third female disagreed: "If you were a crack baby [you might not have a choice]." This discussion continued back and forth until a male student concluded with the following: "[They] don't start out being drug addicts and alcoholics. It's . . . the street that turns them into it. That's their only pleasure. If you don't have nothing else . . . They say they first start drinking just to keep themselves warm. You know, liquor makes you warm inside . . . Then after that it becomes addictive. They can't help it. A lot of people you gave money to were probably drug addicts; you would never know. Ain't nobody gonna say, 'I'm a drug addict, help me out.' So I'm saying, either way, you're helping their cause."

Group 7a's first session produced another variation. A female made the following statement in the midst of a discussion on giving: "Now since I took Mr. Siwek's class, every time I see a homeless person, I have to give money. I'm not going to feel right [if I don't]. I saw this man, like 'I'm homeless.' He had his shoe on the wrong side and it was cold . . . it was very cold. And I said, 'Mom, is this right? Is this man looking me in my face?' So we had three dollars in change. I just grabbed it and threw all the change in his cup. Everyone's not going to feel the same way I do about homeless people, but I just, just get disgusted now. 'Cause people just treat them so bad, like they [were] trash."

The above excerpts display the range of reflections on the moral status of material giving, when benefits were as likely as negative consequences. Other discussions carried reflection a step further. Group 1a in session 3 held the following exchange. One female addressed the use-abuse dilemma by recounting a recent occasion when she saw a homeless person on the corner asking for money. "I gave change one day . . . When I gave it, I was like, I needed that. I gave it to a good cause because maybe she needed it more than I did." A second female elaborated, "That's what I noticed, it's like the more I give . . . the more I get. Like if I give somebody a dollar, when I get home, all of a sudden, my mother gives me $20 or something . . . It's like church; you pay your tithes and God will do good things to you." This general version of the principle that others should be treated as one would want to be treated was expanded on by other discussion groups. Some groups put this principle into religious terms. For example, in group 1a in its first session, a male student said, "I mean, treat [the homeless] the way you want to be treated. You don't want to sit there, you don't want to eat that bowl of soup." A female added, "We are doing the same thing Jesus did when he was here; you know, help others. We learn how to be here for other people instead of being selfish." A second female then added, "It's like she said. You know, Jesus, he helped, he made good with the little he had. And I think that's what we did or we tried to do . . . We tried to feed everyone that was there."

Other statements of this principle appeared in several of the individual essays. For example, student 617 wrote in his third essay: "There is no better feeling in the world than to help your neighbor and stand tall in the eyes of our Lord . . . What [a group of visiting students] didn't know or don't understand is that it isn't whether you want to do this or not. It's your duty as a Christian to serve your neighbor, to love thy neighbor, to treat your neighbor as you would treat God."

Tolerance and Respect for Others

Being directly confronted with homelessness at the kitchen, many students experienced the anthropologist's classic discovery of the *other* (Jahoda 1992). The other refers to people so unfamiliar in one's experience that consciousness of one's presuppositions about life are jostled and thrown open to inspection. The everyday world the observer believed to be natural and took for granted is suddenly challenged so that questions are raised about one's own life in relation to varieties of human existence.

Encountering the other was observed in the St. Francis students, who came to the kitchen with the naive outlooks and parochial experiential backgrounds of 16-year-old high school juniors. For many students, talking to drug addicts, observing knife fights in the kitchen, watching transvestites compete for sexual partners, looking at an underclothed hungry infant, or seeing a schizophrenic elderly woman protecting her soup bowl with darted looks in every direction, were provocative moments of contact with unfamiliar others. Indeed, a recurrent statement, as voiced by student 316, was "I really got a chance to see how the other half lives." As will be shown in chapter 8, alumni from this program cited this aspect of the soup-kitchen experience as a "wake-up call" to the reality of this different and unseemly side of life.

Ignoring insults. Several students noted that some of the homeless diners were rude to them. They made undeserved insults, yelled with impatience, demanded more food, and cursed the students rather than expressing gratitude. Saying that they would ordinarily have retaliated to such remarks, the students instead overlooked the insults because the homeless people were not in normal states of mind. This form of forgiveness, or tolerance, was expressed in several essays and by nearly all discussion groups. It signifies a step beyond the literal practice of reciprocity, via retaliation, to recognition of the principle that not returning an insult is the means for reestablishing a positive relationship (Gouldner 1960).

An example came from student 113 in essay 4: "When I was sweeping the floor, some guy picked up my broom and spit on it because he claims I ran over his foot . . . I just let it go . . . I just laughed it off and continued sweeping." And student 621 wrote that, on being insulted, "we just ignored them."

Group 5a in session 3 had the following discussion. A male asked why others had said the homeless diners were "mean." One student responded, "I didn't say that [but wonder why] sometimes they act like that?" Another male cited a particularly hostile episode, and others who witnessed it agreed. "Yeah, he cursed everybody out. Why are they acting like this?" The second male said, "Because they're homeless. They don't know any better." But another male added, "No, because everybody talks about them and puts them down."

In group 1b's fourth session, a female asked why the homeless were so hostile to them when the students were there to help. A second female said, "I guess I feel like I'd lose a little bit of pride having to be served at a soup kitchen." However, a third female asked, "But why take it out on someone that's helping you?" Two other females answered, "You have to understand it from their point of view" and "I think they're frustrated because some of them feel that nobody's there to help them."

And student 112 wrote in her third essay: "A man in his 40s came in line and started complaining about the soup . . . He started cussing at us so [my friend] gave him a new bowl. I felt sorry for this man because people must have treated him so bad that he takes it out on other people . . . I don't blame him because it's probably not by choice that he comes to the soup kitchen."

Respect for others. These instances of forgiveness, or tolerance, overlap with the showing of respect and may, in fact, have been a form of it. Nevertheless, respect merits its own analysis, as it was defined clearly when students challenged their peers who were showing intolerance of persons who were different than they. One example involved mocking homeless people. In group 4a's fourth discussion, a female said, "Now when I look at homeless people, [they don't] look odd to me. Now it's just like he's another man walking down the street." A male then said, "I don't think I act too much differently. I never, you know, treated them wrong or anything . . . Before I used to just think that they were on drugs or, you know, alcohol; lost their job or something. Now they're homeless." And another female added, "I've changed. My outlook has changed as far as taking a moral stand." She then recounted how she and her friends used to make fun of a homeless woman in their neighborhood. She said, however, "If they did that, I would say something now."

Homosexual males at the kitchen were a repeated target of students' criticism. Many students expressed strong negative feelings about them, even to the point of abhorrence. In session 2, group 4a was discussing transvestites who had come to the kitchen. The student moderator that day asked, "Anyone else like to enlighten on the transvestites?" to which a male responded, "I think a lot of people that go to the soup kitchen got problems . . . They aren't [just] homeless." The leader answered, "I think that everyone has a right to be what they want to be." The male retorted, "We weren't questioning that. We were just saying—"; the leader interrupted, "That's just like saying if you're gay—"; then the male interrupted, "Being gay isn't right or wrong. That's not the point here . . . A lot of homeless people are people that have been released from mental homes and are not mentally here all the way . . . their minds are all messed up. And that's why a lot of them are talking to themselves." The leader said, "But that [doesn't have anything to do] about sexual preference." The male replied, "Yes, if your mind is distorted—" Another female jumped in, "Oh, so when you're gay, your mind is messed up?" The male answered, "I didn't say that." But the second female said, "[But] is that what you're trying to say?"

This kind of challenge to intolerance of homosexuals was echoed in individual essays. A clear case was expressed by student 320, who wrote in his fourth essay: "I don't care what angle you look at it, homosexuality is ungodly and wrong. And I understand the Bible's intentions are not to be taken literally, but the ungodliness of homosexuality is as concrete as the rising and setting of the sun . . . I have never been in close contact with any homosexuals . . . But while I was at the kitchen, a homosexual asked me did I have a nickel. [My friend] had a nickel so she gave it to him. As he began to talk to us, I began to realize that my thinking had been all wrong. I had the same mentality that a red-neck has. I had the same mentality that the Jew-hater has . . . As he talked, I really began to scold myself for thinking the way I did . . . I paid attention to the many marks and bruises that covered his face . . . He doesn't need hatred and abuse from me."

Respect was applied also to others who were different, for instance, prisoners, a point of focus because several ex-prisoners came to the kitchen for meals and social recreation. In group 1b's fourth session, the topic of the death penalty came up, and a female said she thought that the death penalty was wrong but that persons sentenced to death might pay back to society by serving in medical experiments, such as testing for drugs to combat AIDS. A second female yelled, "No, it ain't right." The first female defended her position by saying, "If they're on death row, right, they're supposed to be killed or whatever. So if you test drugs on them, you could be like saving the world." The second female countered satirically by rephrasing the argument, "If you're in jail on death row and I come up to say to you, 'I got an experiment and I want you to take it. Are you going to do it because you're going to die anyway?'" The first female replied, "I wouldn't want to, but I probably wouldn't have any choice. You're in jail. I mean you're on death row." The second female said, "You still have a choice." And a third female added, "You should have a choice."

Compassion

Wuthnow (1991) has identified compassion as the primary moral motive for adult voluntary service. From interviews with rescue squad volunteers to leaders of local PTAs, Wuthnow found that helping others was driven by the desire to create and share a sense of community. For Wuthnow, acts of service are intended to demonstrate that helper and recipient share in a common human struggle. Once this is understood, commitment to assist others in need follows from the implicit principle of reciprocity. In this outlook, people do not act altruistically to achieve self-satisfaction or to relieve another person's pain. Compassion implies that helper and recipient are mutually dependent, live within the same world of vicissitudes and inequalities, and need to share resources if community is to be sustained.

Group 4a's first session provided a clear example of compassion. The group was discussing the possibility that the soup kitchen would have to be closed because it would be torn down for construction of a commercial structure. Someone mentioned the term *gentrification,* and this provoked a discussion about the juxtaposition of wealth and poverty in Washington. A female student concluded this discussion with the following commentary: "Why are these people trying to beautify the area? Where do they think these people that aren't as lucky going to go? They go where they can be helped and where they're going to be fed . . . [The developers] don't know what the [homeless] are going through . . . I don't think they can put themselves in that place because they don't really know what the other people are going through. I don't think they care. They really don't care."

Other articulations of compassion were expressed in individual essays. One such essay was written after student 123's fourth and last scheduled assignment at the kitchen. On this visit, he had the opportunity to go into the dining area to talk with the diners, and he was invited to join a group that was playing cards. He described his experience: "Then I finally got to play. I lost, but it wasn't about winning or losing, it was about just showing that you cared, not just that you cared, but you cared enough that you came to them and they didn't [have to] come to you. I mean at that moment we were just people, people that had something in common."

A similar expression occurred in group 3a's second discussion about reasons for helping the homeless. A female student said, "I think a lot of people do it out of guilt or whatever. And I don't think that's the right reason to do it. I think the right reason . . . is because you have a passion to help the homeless and truly live a life according to what God has taught us. I don't think you should do it out of guilt, because if you do, eventually that desire . . . is going to wear off." A male student added, "I think people are motivated to help the homeless because they figure it's the right thing to do."

Student 508's third essay expressed clearly that society consists in a succession of generations, precisely in the sense that Erikson hoped youth would comprehend. "Working at the kitchen is a great experience for people of the age of 14 or older. It helps you appreciate what you were put on earth for. You were put on earth for a reason; you are here to help people who can't help themselves or get a job . . . You should want a better future for the next generation of younger children who want to make it in society."

In his third essay, student 509 wrote: "It is very sad and upsetting out in the real world [where] you see people on the street everyday. How could this happen? When are we going to realize that these people need help? . . . Sometimes I wonder to myself, do people care?"

In the beginning of the year, students were surprised by the variety of people they saw at the soup kitchen. This frequently led to discussions about who was and who was not homeless and arguments about how deserving these contested diners were. After students' initial visit to the kitchen, segments of discussions were devoted to sorting out who the homeless are (see chapter 4) and who deserves to receive free meals. Arguments were instigated by seeing diners who wore new and expensive clothes or having to listen to diners' complaints about the quality of the food.

The usual argument began with an observation, for example, that some diners wore expensive athletic jackets or leather coats. This was typically followed by a chorus of additional examples from other students. Once the negative examples started to flow and an image of the diners as fakes and cheats gained momentum, it took a strong intervention to turn discussion around toward a compassionate conclusion. But this was done repeatedly when one or more students used the following tactic. First, the facts of the preceding discussion were admitted. Then the student inserted an admonishing request to consider an alternate, more compassionate interpretation of the facts. This use of compassion goes beyond empathy, because of its strategic role in the context of argument. It was used to say to the group that homeless people should not be judged unfairly and not be held to standards that the students themselves did not meet. In this regard, compassion was powerful enough to shift the entire group's outlook and get the group to stop judging the homeless stereotypically, thereby allowing students to look on them as diverse people who vary among themselves as the students themselves differed from one another.

The examples now presented are taken from the first discussion sessions, when students were initially coming to grips with meeting the homeless. Group 1a shared observations of three males who stood out at the kitchen because they were young, between 20 and 25, and well dressed. One of this trio tried to get a date with one of the St. Francis females. He was carrying a new and expensive sports bag and wearing $100 sneakers. One student asked, "What's going on here?" A second student suggested there should be a supervisor at the door to keep out people who were not homeless and could afford to buy meals. After other confirming observations were added, a female student intervened by shifting the frame with a new line of thinking: "Sometimes they['re] dressed up 'cause somebody gave it to them; [they] feel sorry for them." This was then rearticulated by a second female: "In my family whenever we have clothes that we don't want anymore or whatever, we try to put it out somewhere, [people] will eventually take it, you know, [or we] give it out to people . . . So you can't really look at a person's clothes and say, 'Well, they have money, they have tennis shoes—Reebok or something like that.'"

Group 4a had a nearly identical discussion when one student noted that a few diners at the kitchen carried beepers and wore expensive sneakers and warm-up jackets. Other students added they saw a man in a three-piece suit, a security guard, and a postal worker in the eating line. As this list became longer, a female interrupted to warn the group not to judge the people they saw too hastily. Regarding people in uniforms, she said, "That could be the only outfit they had. Like they worked as a security guard and they kept on wearing it every day."

Students were also bothered by complaints made by the homeless diners (see the section above on tolerance). In group 3a, a female student told about a man who complained about the food, saying that the man ought to be grateful. However, she checked herself by adding, "But I guess that's just human." A second female entered the discussion by saying, "That's what I was thinking . . . if you don't have something, why would you, you know, complain a lot?" The first female said, "But I guess they figure since they finally getting something, they want it right." A male then said, "I mean, treat them the way you want to be treated." MY asked, "So what did you say to this guy?" The first female answered, "'It's OK.' He had already eaten it, that's what I don't understand. But he was just coming back and coming back. And then I thought, well maybe he just real hungry. [I told him to take an extra apple] . . . He kept filling up his bag with apples . . . I guess that's the way a lot of people on the street are. If you find something, you take as much as you can. I guess like *we* do in life."

Agency and Responsibility

A key to moral identity is establishing one's capacity as a social agent who has responsibility to secure a better, more just and compassionate society. Agency was implied in the above excerpts when students tried to shift trains of thinking from a judgmental direction to a more compassionate mode of tolerance and respect. Such efforts showed that students felt responsibility to the homeless and to their peers. They wanted to show their peers that their observations, despite being factual, had moral implications.

We now look at agency and responsibility from another angle by assessing statements that signify that students were beginning to incorporate moral agency into their identities. The chief distinguishing mark of these excerpts is that students explicitly connected their current experience at the soup kitchen with the lives they projected for themselves in the future.

For example, student 509 wrote in his third essay: "Working at the soup kitchen has been a good experience but I still can't help feel worthless and powerless to change the situation . . . I don't leave the soup kitchen feeling good . . . I feel helpless and guilty. I feel guilty because I want the people who come to the soup kitchen to have a normal life . . . When I serve the soup, I don't know what to say. I feel I have a responsibility to save them, but I can't . . . Life was not intended to be sustained, it was meant to be lived. The people at the soup kitchen should be out living life to its fullest but they can't."

In her third essay, student 425 wrote: "Why am I so fortunate and they aren't? I got up to play with a girl that was sitting eating a saltine cracker . . . What was her future to be like? I don't think she had a proper home because she was wrapped in layers and layers of clothes. Her hands were as cold as ice and wrinkled with dryness . . . My future will be dedicated to children and homelessness . . . I'm not just saying [this] to impress you, but because it is a promise I have made to myself."

Student 620 in his final essay wrote: "The people I saw this day were playing cards, joking around, just like a family picnic. It is hard to swallow that these people are just like you and me. The only difference is when I go home I'm able to have a warm meal and hot shower . . . Sometimes I take things for granted and think of that as acceptable. The more I look at myself I realize how much I need to change."

These sentiments were also expressed during discussions and thus had the potential to become emblematic symbols that others in the group could adopt. In group 5b's third session, a male student stated, "You gotta incorporate it into your life. I mean, you're right, not everybody's gonna take something from [this course] with them. It's not gonna make a difference for some people. But for [other] people this could be the start of—in the future, if they become successful, looking back and saying, there are people out there who need [help]."

Justice with Compassion

Rather than trying to fit results into one major theory of morality, we organized the present chapter around basic elements or principles that can fit a general theoretical perspective. We still had difficulty sorting statements into tightly bound categories, because students often coupled two or more categories in their narratives. We could not always say exactly where reciprocity or compassion ended, for example, and agency or responsibility began.

An advantage of service was that it gave students experience in applying moral concepts to real people in real situations. Apropos Erikson's notion of industry, these actions allowed students to assess themselves as moral actors. It follows, then, that many students used these data to project themselves forward in time to adulthood when they would become moral actors in a wider societal context (cf. chapter 5). These projections were grounded in a tested capacity to help others that was made possible through service at the kitchen. To imagine being able to help others and being part of a solution to social problems is an obvious sign that students were beginning to integrate morality into their emerging definitions of self.

The concept of compassion was introduced as a supraordinate category that captured the breadth of students' moral outlooks better than formal notions such as protecting personal rights. By sympathetically taking the perspective of homeless people, people on welfare, prisoners, transvestites, and others, students acknowledged that they and these others share a common humanity. The well-being of others was as important as, and perhaps dependent on, students' own well-being. As Wuthnow argued, the driving motive to help others is based on an understanding that people are interdependent and thus in need of mutual compassion.

Compassion differs from justice, which deals with formal rights, equality, and the like (e.g., Kohlberg 1969). Compassion implies that individuals and society are linked via shared existence and interdependence. It is probably more psychological and less based on deliberative logic. This view does not preempt the importance of rights, equality, and so on but combines with it, in the coupling of justice with goodwill. The following excerpts exemplify this combination.

In group 5a's first session, a male student said, "First of all, I think this program should be incorporated into, like, the regular school curriculum in public schools . . . You can't just teach somebody to be Christian or you can't teach everybody Catholicism . . . But this course is *social justice,* the whole society and justice within that society. So everyone can relate to that. Everyone wants the society . . . to be really good." A second male agreed, "I didn't know this was a religion course." But a third male asked the first, "What are you getting at?" The second male answered, "I think I know what he's trying to say." And the first male explained, "What I'm saying is that everyone will sort of agree that because it's not just Catholicism, or whatever. And no one can really get offended by helping other people . . . Social justice is about the well-being of the whole society."

The same concept was expressed in student 402's fourth essay: "[We] need to realize that these people no matter what the creed, color, or race, or what have they, they are considered people. I wouldn't want to eat anything from a rusty tray, no matter how hungry I was . . . I'm being grateful for what I have and to know that someone cares for me . . . These people are like you and me, but the only difference is that they have to sleep in the cold, on hard, cold cement, and we with our eyes closed on soft beds . . . We all should take a moral stand to what's happening to our community and try as decent human beings to fix up our gift from God."

Finally, student 309 in her fourth essay wrote: "But it is my personal responsibility to change [society]. Having poor people is virtually inevitable, but the real task is to have people view them as human. If money is the American dream, then America has killed the dream that I and many others have dreamed . . . The people at the kitchen are the most humble and reserved people I've seen. Throughout their lives they have been allotted few excess[es] yet they still are able to face tomorrow, tomorrow with the moon and the skies laughing at them, the sun turning its back, the dust blowing in their eyes. Yet some of them still have hope. Oddly, this time I noticed a smell. I smelt the rotten people in the world . . . I smelt injustice. I smelt the indifference."

Conclusion

This and chapter 5 were designed to illustrate how service at the soup kitchen provoked awareness of political and moral dimensions and allowed students to perceive themselves as political and moral agents with responsibility to make society a better place. From the perspective of politics, students manifested the characteristics desired of mature citizens in a democratic society. From a moral perspective, students expressed compassion for others, a belief in interdependence, and hope for a society in which justice prevailed for all.

We recognize that individual statements and discursive exchanges do not prove anything definite about the program's success. Nevertheless, we propose that they demonstrate what can be accomplished in a service program of this type. Useful service to people in need emboldens students to imagine a better society without homelessness and where less fortunate people of all kinds would receive respect and fair treatment.

The statements we reviewed may appear naive about the causes of social problems and idealistic about their correction. But the statements are clearly coherent with a broad ideology that makes social justice its primary aim and demands responsible action from everyone, even adolescents, to achieve that aim. This reflects the kind of ideology that Erikson believes the younger generation needs in order to move ahead in the identity process. Youth need to have ideals worth working toward that transcend themselves and promise to link an incomplete but hopeful past with an attainable and better future.

The excerpts provide only brief glimpses into the thinking of these students, but they are sufficient to show how service can stimulate and support identity development. There is no way to tell whether the reflections cited here will be the building blocks for lifelong development. They are, however, ideas on which students can build as they continue in the identity process. This foundation is essential for the political and moral individuals society desires. We do not argue that these outcomes follow only from this particular program, but we offer this program as a clear example of how to arouse the identity search and equip it with a gyroscope these students can use as a guide to political maturity and enduring moral resolve as they move ahead to adulthood.

CHAPTER SEVEN

On Being a Black American

Chapters 4–6 looked at ways service at the soup kitchen and participation in the social justice course stimulated students to reflect on homelessness, moral responsibility, and political processes. In this chapter, we show how, in discussing these topics, students addressed ideas about their identity as Black adolescents. Throughout the year, students made frequent references, especially in group discussions, to the meaning of being Black. They brought up race in general terms and addressed specifically what life was like for them as Black American teenagers in the 1990s. Students questioned the kind of political and moral lives they will lead from the perspective of belonging to a minority group with a complex history of social oppression and moral fortitude.

It is not surprising that students connected their experiences at the soup kitchen with ideas about their own ethnic identity. Several researchers have reported a strong link between the processes of politicization and consciousness of ethnic identity (e.g., Verba and Nie 1972; Garcia 1982). Moreover, this connection has been found to be particularly strong among Black Americans (Phinney 1990). A central part of the process of understanding who one is as a Black American entails coming to grips with political and social history.

Cross's writings (1995a, 1995b) on the process of developing Black consciousness offer a helpful way of describing the influence of service experience on students' sense of Black identity. Cross uses the term *encounter* to describe a single moment or series of small moments that provoke reflection on the meaning of one's membership within a racial or ethnic group and that encourage the reshaping of one's worldview. Examples of a single dramatic encounter include the assassination of Martin Luther King Jr. and the initial verdict dismissing charges against the police officers charged with beating Rodney King. Other examples offered by Cross are discussions with family and friends on the meaning of Blackness, and being personally assaulted or having a friend assaulted in a racial incident.

For many St. Francis students, the social justice course and service at the soup kitchen represented an encounter. Seeing a stream of young Black men pour into the soup kitchen for hot chicken soup at 9:30 in the morning or seeing a relative wait in line for food took some students aback. They responded by reflecting on the implications for their own minority status with reference to treatment of other people and prospects for their own lives. For some students, these reflections were part of an ongoing process of heightened consciousness of Black identity. Cross (1995a) posits that this process in childhood and adolescence is most likely encouraged by family members who stress Black consciousness and are active in Black-oriented cultural, social, or political activities. For other students, specific soup-kitchen or classroom experiences may represent a pivotal point in thinking about the connections between race and identity. Whether service at the soup kitchen was one of a series of moments or marked a unique turning point for the students, it is worth considering how the issue of Blackness surfaced repeatedly in accounts of incidents at the kitchen and conversations in the classroom and discussion groups.

Descriptions of Service at the Soup Kitchen

In writing and talking about their experiences at the soup kitchen, students' descriptions of the people they served and of other volunteers often brought up racial issues. In their essays, students noted how their experiences contradicted racial stereotypes about who is homeless. For example, student 109 wrote in his first essay: "They were all there, black, white, Hispanic, Japanese, all ethnic groups, cultures, and sexes. It just proves homelessness is a plague that doesn't give a damn what race you are." In a similar vein, student 529 wrote in her third essay: "Any type of person can be put into the position that they have to go to the soup kitchen young, old, black, white, Hispanic, dark skin, light skin, black hair, white hair, clean faces, dirty faces, suits, ties, sweatshirts, beards, mustaches, any types and all types they are."

In group discussions, students shared views that challenged stereotypes of the homeless and Blacks. An example comes from the first meeting of group 3b, in which three students built upon each other's ideas about preconceptions and stereotypes of who is homeless. To begin, a female student said, "Well when you say 'homeless people,' I mean not me necessarily, but other people automatically think that you are talking about Black people when you say, 'homeless.'" A second female elaborated, "Because we are supposed to come from the ghetto and not have a lot of stuff and the White people are supposed to come from nice neighborhoods." A male student then added, "Beverly Hills. You see what most people don't realize is that we are, I mean Black people are a minority."

Another example comes from the second meeting of group 3a. This exchange began when a female student described some volunteers from out of town who were at the kitchen on her day of service. She recounted, "When I went, there was [a group of student volunteers] from North Carolina . . . I was serving soup with the teacher. She seemed sort of racist to me . . . A few White people came in and, like, she was saying, like she could understand how Black people could do something like this . . . It was like 'Oh, you're better than this.'" A second female asked, "Do you think that's because she didn't know? It's just that she hadn't thought that a White person shouldn't be homeless or something like that? Do you think that it's something you're taught, or do you think it's something that, you know, she just thought of?" The first student responded, "I just think she thought it was going to be Black people. She acted really surprised when she saw White people." At this point, a third student entered the conversation to draw a conclusion from what had been said: "I think a lot of people don't realize that homelessness is not a situation of color. It's a situation that needs to be dealt with."

A notable aspect of this exchange is students' attempts to understand the attitudes of White volunteers. On any given day, in addition to the students from St. Francis, there were also volunteers from other area schools or out of town. Most of these volunteers were White. For example, one group of semiregular volunteers came from an elite parochial high school. In discussion groups, St. Francis students sometimes criticized these students, referred to as "the White kids," for not working hard enough or for being scared to interact with the homeless. An evident part of this criticism was the comparison favoring St. Francis students, who were more hardworking and caring than other volunteers. This comparison helped to affirm the special status of the St. Francis students. It is understandable that students would want to emphasize the strengths of their school in comparison to the several elite parochial schools in the area. The St. Francis students knew that these other schools were predominately White and had better financial resources and academic reputations. To build themselves up, students were outspoken in their pride for the traditions of St. Francis, which included service to the community and a top-notch football team which regularly beat the other schools' teams.

At the same time that students were evaluating racial stereotypes of the homeless, students also revealed increased awareness of the vulnerability of Blacks, particularly Black youth, to homelessness. They noted that a sizable group of people served at the kitchen were Black. For example, student 124 wrote in her first essay: "There were people of all walks of life, Hispanics, Caucasians, Koreans, and most of all African Americans." In another instance, student 108 wrote in her first essay: "I also never realized how many young Black men were frequent visitors. Men, that if I saw on the street, I would never have imagined that they needed to eat at a soup kitchen."

Discussion groups also revealed connections between homelessness and Blacks. In one example from the first meeting of discussion group 4a, a student made the following comment regarding the recent history of gentrification in DC: "I mean not just with homeless people. It happens with everybody. Like Georgetown was a residential Black place. Then they moved all the Black people out. So it's White people. Now it's what you call a preppie town in the middle of DC, right? It's the same thing. They're going to move the homeless out, upscale it."

These examples capture the complex ways that racial issues were brought up in students' descriptions of the soup kitchen. While service at the soup kitchen challenged students to reflect on racial stereotypes of the homeless, students also recognized that a sizable proportion of homeless at the soup kitchen were Black. The number of Blacks in line was not surprising in a city with a wide majority of Blacks. However, students had to work through the idea that, although many homeless in DC are Black, homeless people both in DC and elsewhere can be of any race. Students also had to contend with an increased sense of vulnerability as they met homeless Black youth who had lived in their neighborhood or graduated from parochial school. Perhaps this vulnerability helps to explain why students made efforts to build themselves up by criticizing White volunteers. For these youth, the process of identity development entailed fitting themselves within an interracial social order while protecting and maintaining a sense of ethnic pride.

Messages about Blackness in the Classroom

Students often talked about racial aspects of the curriculum and Mr. Siwek's classroom comments in their discussion groups. These discussions occurred as students ranged from recounting specific soup-kitchen experiences to examining the meaning of these experiences for their education and their future careers. We identified four recurrent themes that exemplify how racial issues were brought up in the classroom. These are (1) Mr. Siwek's comments about his being White, (2) emphasis of Black role models, (3) criticism of Black public figures who do not take moral stands, and (4) expectation of students' response to events with racial implications. In the examples below, group 3a appears four times. Their disproportionate representation was consciously chosen because they gave clear and concise examples of major points.

A White Man Teaching Social Justice to Black Youth

Mr. Siwek was direct about his being a White man teaching Black youth. Throughout the year, he made serious comments but also joked about the fact he was White. For example, he responded to a video showing a White woman at a town meeting arguing against a homeless shelter by saying, "Do you know how I feel when I see this? It makes me want to vomit. It makes me ashamed to be White and to be American." In a more lighthearted instance, Siwek joked to the class when they laughed because he lost his glasses: "Why are you laughing? White people have feelings too." He used these spontaneous remarks to make students recognize their stereotypes of Whites and present himself as different from these stereotypes. Much of this process was done through humor and was greeted with laughter or smirks. In an example from Siwek's description of the awards night at the end of the year, he said, "There are 25 awards. I win the award for Whitest person in the course. I also win Whitest person who tries to be Black."

An important question to address is whether Siwek's self-presentation helped weaken students' stereotypes of White people or encouraged students to think of him as different from other White people. In group 3a's third meeting, students exchanged views pertinent to this issue. One female student began by saying, "I don't know if he [makes jokes about White people] to loosen us up or to make us laugh or whatever, but I mean we don't go around talking about how White people

have big noses . . . I don't know why he does it." Another female student responded by saying, "I think he kind of does it to make us understand that, all right 'I'm White, but I'm trying to help you all to
understand that, even though I'm White, I understand what's going
on out here.'" A male student elaborated, "To make up for what happened years ago. To bring us all together instead of being separate."
The second student continued, "Somebody asked, 'Why is it that you
always pick on Black people who have money like M. C. Hammer and
Michael Jordan?' And he said, 'Because you don't expect it from
White people, but it would seem like the Black people . . . would help
their own people out.' And that kind of made me think he . . . was kind
of . . . against White people . . . But then he turns around and shows
us Martin Luther King and he's saying not to hate the White man but
to be friends with him . . . I don't think that Siwek hates White people
because he's White . . . He can't deny that, but it's just that he hates
what White people have done." Another male student then entered
the conversation by saying, "He's all right for a White person. He's the
first I've ever been around and talked to."

Emphasis of Black Role Models

A central part of the curriculum included presentations on Black
people who have served their communities or dedicated their lives to
social justice. These people were offered as role models for the students
and were referred to as authoritative resources in support of Siwek's
statements in class. Siwek emphasized the names of Black public officials and community leaders such as Vernon Jordan, Kweisi Mfume,
Marion Wright Edelman, and Thurgood Marshall. He also included
course readings on athletes and entertainers, such as Arthur Ashe and
Stevie Wonder, who have taken stands for social justice. Illustrating this
approach, Siwek spent much of the second day of class reading a tribute
to the recently deceased Boston Celtic basketball star, Reggie Lewis.
The tribute focused on Lewis's community service such as distributing
turkeys in his childhood neighborhood each Christmas. Referring to
this tribute, Siwek asked: "Why do I like this article?" and a student
responded, "Because he gave back to his community." Siwek said,
"That's right," and drew on the board: Have → Have Not.

Martin Luther King Jr. was a pivotal authoritative figure in the
class. For example, in talking about the continued prevalence of racial
conflict in the United States in the 1990s, Siwek advocated nonviolent

reform and inclusion by stating, "I warn you not to be sucked in by rage . . . Skin color should be no more important than the color of my eyes and I know that's easy to say as a White person because I haven't been subjected. But Martin Luther King was subjected to that rage, and his goal was to create the 'Beloved Community' for everyone." On another occasion, Siwek again brought up King as a role model for the students: "He lived way ahead of his time. When Martin Luther King loves the man who calls him 'nigger,' the world leaps forward. Don't buy into primitive behavior."

The students appreciated Siwek's efforts to emphasize the contributions of Blacks, and, for the most part, they wanted more Black history in the school curriculum. However, there were also a few students who were concerned about emphasizing the past because they feared it might impede the future. An example occurred in group 3a's fourth meeting when a conversation about the Nation of Islam led MY to ask, "Do you learn about Malcolm X in school?" A male student replied, "Outside of Mr. Siwek, I mean that's it." A female student added, "[Mr. Siwek's assignment] was the only Black thing we read about. We don't read nothing Black [except also for] the Harlem Renaissance." A second female agreed, "That's it," but then a second male introduced a dissenting opinion: "I don't think we need to read stuff about it . . . We need to stop dwelling on the past all of the time and worry about tomorrow." The first male challenged this perspective: "Martin Luther King is tomorrow."

The last two comments acknowledge implicitly that "something needs to be done" to improve the conditions of Black Americans and represent two common positions on how change will come about. One student worried that emphasizing negative events of the past will paralyze Blacks' ability to move into the future. He wanted to focus on the present and the ability of individuals to confront challenges. The other student viewed the past in a different way. He saw events in U.S. Black history not solely in terms of oppression, but also in terms of moral fortitude as embodied by Martin Luther King. He believed that, to move ahead, Black youth need to learn and draw strength from the past.

Criticism of Some Black Public Figures

Mr. Siwek not only presented Black role models for the students, but also directed pointed criticism toward Black public figures who he believed were not helping those in need. Over the year, he repeatedly criticized celebrities such as basketball star Michael Jordan and rapper M. C. Hammer for being motivated by greed. He typically made these criticisms by mentioning celebrities' names at moments when he was making a point about the students' responsibility to respond to injustice. For example, in talking about the upcoming first trip to the soup kitchen, Siwek said, "You can't buy the feeling of giving someone a bowl of soup. Michael Jordan can't buy that." In another example, he introduced a video about a program in Harlem that gives young men construction skills and a chance to earn a graduation equivalency diploma (GED) by saying, "People like Hammer think it's chic to live in a $20 million home. Do you know what we could do with this money?"

Although many students reacted strongly to Siwek's criticisms, they usually did not voice their reaction in class but waited until the discussion group. Discussions of celebrities did not center on Siwek's criticisms of members of the Black community, but rather on the reasonableness of expecting a rich person to help those who have less. A few students were outspoken in support or opposition to these criticisms. Generally, students felt uncomfortable about judging other people's actions. Several students specifically spoke about their plans to be doctors or lawyers one day, when they would have to confront the issue of whether and how to "give back."

Here are examples of debates about Michael Jordan. During group 4a's first meeting, students struggled to understand Mr. Siwek's comments about celebrities. One female student said, "[Mr. Siwek] takes things out on people who have money . . . saying like, 'It's their fault. Why can't Michael Jordan build that complex across from the stadium?' I don't know. But it's not Michael Jordan's fault that everybody's out there." A second female countered by saying, "Mr. Siwek's not saying that it's Michael Jordan's fault." A male student then said, "Michael Jordan does some things. Siwek is just taking it out of context." In another example from group 3a's second meeting, a male student defended Michael Jordan by saying, "He didn't just wake up and be Michael Jordan. He had to work hard." A female student responded, "He has to work hard to be where he's at, but look at all the other people. A lot of homeless people work hard, but look where they're at." The first student replied, "That not his fault," and the second student countered, "That's not his fault, but that's his obligation."

These two excerpts show students grappling with the issues of "context" and "obligation" in critiquing Siwek's comments and understanding human action. The discussion in the first excerpt ended when one student brought up the notion of evaluating someone out of context. Is it fair for Siwek to disregard someone's background and life experiences and to expect them to perform volunteer work just because they are financially successful? A part of the contextual argument was whether Siwek really knew about the life of a person like Michael Jordan. Does he know whether Michael Jordan helps the community or not? Students believed that these specific questions were important and did not like the idea of Siwek's making symbolic points by referring to specific individuals.

The second discussion ended when a student refocused the conversation from blame to obligation. For some students, this was a way of avoiding judgments and emphasizing the positive. This shifting of the conversation also made it more personal in terms of what students understood to be their own obligations. When students introduced the notion of obligation, they were open to being challenged by their peers about their own motivations and actions in the present and future.

Response to Events with Racial Implications

Mr. Siwek also criticized Black public figures who he thought followed an agenda of racial divisiveness. A key event that occurred during the year of the study was a speech by Khalid Muhammed, a former aide to Louis Farrakhan of the Nation of Islam, at Howard University. This speech earned media attention because it included statements critical of Jews, Catholics, Whites, and the media. In particular, Muhammed was perceived as pitting Blacks against Jews for arguing that Blacks have suffered far worse than Jews in the Black holocaust perpetrated in the United States, a holocaust that has never been formally recognized. Siwek responded to this event by showing a video of Muhammed's speech to the class without comment and on the next day of class showing them another video that he had compiled by juxtaposing statements from Muhammed's speech with statements by Martin Luther King Jr. and pictures of the Holocaust. He then stated to the class: "If the gates of oppression are never open they will blow up. Whether they should or shouldn't is irrelevant. People who are oppressed will, but, look at me, that was not the message of Martin Luther King or Desmond Tutu. They didn't say, 'Blow sky high' . . . Just because Black people have suffered does not mean no one else has. That Ireland hasn't been oppressed for 700 years by the British . . . Would it have been too much for Farrakhan's aide to walk out of the Holocaust Museum and say, 'These people have suffered too'?" This case illustrates that Siwek did not shy away from controversial events concerning race and his pedagogical method of confronting racism with alternative behaviors.

Another moment during the course when an alternative response was offered occurred when the Middle East Peace Accord was signed in fall 1993. Siwek tried to generalize its significance with reference to violence and racial conflict in the United States. He said, "A larger vision than just revenge. Violence getting us nowhere is the theme of *Menace II Society* [1993 film set in south central Los Angeles]. We have to go in a new direction. This can be done with the Crips and the Bloods, the Blacks and Koreans."

In discussion groups, students brought up the Nation of Islam and Khalid Muhammed and voiced a range of responses. In concurrence with Siwek, many students were opposed to the inflammatory rhetoric of both Khalid Muhammed and Louis Farrakhan. At the same time, they did not dismiss the importance of the Nation of Islam in its service to Black communities, activities that Siwek did not bring up in class. An example of criticism for the Nation of Islam comes from group 3a's fourth meeting, when one male student said, "I think [Khalid Muhammed] was totally wrong and I'm against Farrakhan." A second male elaborated, "What [the Muslims] are doing is just going to make it worse for us . . . They're talking about killing White people. That's going to be more Black people in jail making it worse." The first student then added, "They're supposed to be teaching us to uprise with, you know, knowledge. But they're trying to teach us that while they uprise with their fists."

In discussion group 3b's fourth meeting, students voiced both criticism and praise. Focusing on the speech at Howard University, a male student said, "Khalid Muhammed, he ain't got no real friends. He's just a speaker." A second male offered, "He's a good motivator," but a female student cut him off, saying, "That's ignorant. All that name calling was ignorant." Later in the conversation students recounted some of the positive aspects of the Nation of Islam. A male student said, "If you're a brother, they're going to look out for you." A female student concurred, "They bring Black males together," and another male student added, "They stand up for themselves." The female student continued, "They pull themselves in, they educate them." A third male said, "They take over the drug neighborhoods and stuff," and a second female said, "They unify each other. Instead of fighting, they'll be educated."

This last excerpt shows students' ability to examine events from more than one perspective. Students did not uniformly accept or reject Siwek's position; rather, they identified positive and negative aspects and struggled to come to an overall conclusion. They disliked Muhammed's rhetoric, but they approved of the Nation of Islam's efforts to strengthen Black inner-city communities. In a similar fashion, they believed that Michael Jordan could do more for social justice, but they felt everyone could do more and it was wrong to judge another person without knowing the facts.

It is striking how wary students were of oversimplifying issues concerning race in the discussion groups. Christian principles, the high expectations that students had for themselves, and personal experiences promoted caution in evaluating the actions of others. On several occasions, students articulated a variation of the maxim that "only God can judge the actions of others." In addition, many students expected to be professionally successful and, therefore, in a position in the future where they might be judged by others. Finally, students' hesitancy to oversimplify issues concerning race reflects the influence of important individuals in the students' lives. In contrast to Mr. Siwek's views, some parents and peers of students were supportive of Black nationalism and opposed any criticism of Black material success. For example, several students knew people, including relatives, who attended Muhammed's speech at Howard University.

Understanding Their Lives as Black Americans

Students' understanding of the meaning of being Black Americans was a central issue directly addressed in discussion groups. Discussions sometimes took the form of examining negative societal images of Blacks, particularly Black youth. At other times, discussions focused on the past experiences of family members and students' ideas about their own generational identity. Examples from these discussions show how students reflected on the historical framework for their Black identity. We connect this developing sense of identity to students' service experience.

Negative Societal Images of Blacks

Over the year, students often talked about negative societal images of
Blacks. In one extended debate from the first meeting of group 3b,
students argued heatedly with a student who used the term *turning
Black* to describe the behavior of welfare recipients at the post office
when they fail to receive their monthly check. She stated, "People
come in there and they start turning Black on everybody and just
going off on the whole post office." A male student interrupted her,
"What do you mean 'turning Black?' . . . Do you mean Black like ignorant now? . . . What is 'acting Black?' What is it? I have to act like a
hoodlum?" A second female student interjected, "And then when
Black folk act intelligent, they—" "Oh, you're acting White," the male
student said to complete her comment. Another male student then
stated, "If you're Black, you don't need to *act* Black."

Students also brought up negative racial images when they talked
about drugs, crime, and housing. This connection was made because
students were aware that the media often linked social problems and
race. Students denounced this viewpoint and in the process often articulated an oppositional perspective to Whites. For example, in talking about drug legalization in group 5a's third discussion, one male
student voiced the perspective, "You know why they all don't want us to
smoke [marijuana]? Because they fear when we smoke it, we spread it
over to the suburbs where they are living . . . The only way they look at
it is how it affects them . . . Cause I know back in the 60s, I've seen a
whole bunch of tapes with all these White people smoking marijuana
and there were cops standing right there and they never said something to them. If you catch a Black person smoking marijuana, now
they'll take you to jail real quick."

In another example, students talked about changes in their school
and perceptions of Black youth. This excerpt, from group 5b's third
discussion, began when MY asked the students what they thought was
going to happen to St. Francis in the next few years. A female student
responded, "I think it's gonna be all White because the tuition keeps
going up and if you look at it. What? How many students have been
thrown out of St. Francis this year? A lot. Because . . . the mentality for
the Black youth is that they don't care, and all they're concerned
about is drugs." A second female replied, "It ain't about you don't have
the money. I don't think it's gonna be all White." The first female responded, "I think it is. They want to raise the tuition, they won't have

so many problems." A third female then supported the second by say-ing, "They raising the tuition because they keep making changes and stuff, putting in new windows. That's why they need money. I don't think it'll be all White because no schools that I know of. Listen, no school that was all White previously, that's like majority Black now has ever switched back over like that. Listen. And another thing is that a lot of White people are moving out of DC now."

These excerpts elaborate the perspective that White society views Blacks negatively and does not care about their fate. The final excerpt is particularly disturbing in articulating students' belief that society sees Black youth as troublemakers with whom Whites do not want to attend school or live.

Experiences of Family Members

Trying to understand issues of social justice afforded the opportunity for students to bring up family members' experiences of both hard-ship and success. Students were aware of their family history as it con-nected to the history of the civil rights movement and, for some, the opening up of opportunities. For example, in group 4a's fourth meet-ing, students talked about whether government money should be spent on memorials. A female student supported the Vietnam Memo-rial by saying, "It was for poor people. They had no choice. I mean not everybody can afford to go to Canada. Not everybody can afford for their rich parents to support them. They had no choice, people were drafted . . . My mother's fiancé was drafted. He was poor and Black and they sent him over there and he had no choice in the matter. So yes, you should honor him."

Later in the same group, a sense of generational awareness emerged again as students debated the causes of racial segregation. A female student commented, "My grandmother's family was real, real poor but she did something . . . Her family decided to get together and buy all these little lots up and make money and build stores . . . If she hadn't done that, generation after generation . . . I could be living in the ghetto." Not all students agreed with this interpretation and a male student responded by saying, "No, I think a lot [of segregation has] to do with Blacks, a lot of Blacks they have negative, you know, images of Whites and Whites have negative images of Blacks, so Blacks generally tend to want to live with other Blacks and Whites generally want to live with, um, other Whites. And that's just the way it is."

In a third example, students elaborated upon each other's descriptions of the shared experiences of their parents and grandparents. They also revealed awareness of new challenges facing their generation. This series of exchanges in group 3a's final meeting was initiated when a student mentioned how he disliked the civil rights videos depicting racial violence that Mr. Siwek showed in class. The male student said, "I don't really like it when he [shows] us racist videos about White people beating up Black people . . . I already told him one day that we already know about struggle and we don't need to be watching this and that. And he got an attitude or something, like he struggled too in all of this. I ain't never known a White person who struggled through with all of this." A female student interjected, "And he shows the videos like it's gonna be a big surprise for us. But our parents and our grandparents are the ones who had to live through that so it's not gonna be like 'Oh wow,' to us, because we already know about it." Another female student continued, "It can't compare to what our parents and what our grandparents went through, but we got our own struggle now growing up now. I mean I think right now [is] a worse time to be a teenager, you can't hardly do nothing because . . . it's just taking our childhood away."

Generational Awareness

Excerpts from discussions of both racial images and experiences of family members include interpretations of negative aspects of students' experience as a generation of Black Americans. Students were aware of media images of Blacks as delinquents, and throughout the year, there were outrageous reminders of the challenges students faced. In one example, two male students with good grades and church affiliations were leaving a movie theater and were detained and frisked by the police because they were searching for a "Black male youth" who had mugged somebody.

Another example of the burden some students felt was provided when students had to cope with expulsion of a student who had a gun in his car in the school parking lot. Mr. Siwek let the students talk about the incident during a class. One female tearfully said, "Our generation is all about retaliation. Sometimes I'm so scared. Now it's to the point that I don't care." Siwek responded, "Will you just look around you. Are you drowning in a wave and you are going to let it surround you?" The same female replied, "Most people, I'm not saying you, Mr.

Siwek, they put us down. They don't help us. We need help." Another female continued, "You are going to do what you can," then quoting a statistic from a course reading, she added, "'Middle age for Black men is 25.'"

We offer these examples not to be alarmist, but because a critical step in the development of Black consciousness is a realistic assessment of the current condition of Blacks in the United States. Supporting this point, West (1993) argues that, while a sense of nihilism seems to pervade the social and political lives of many Black Americans in the 1990s, both the conservative and the liberal analysts have failed to acknowledge and confront this nihilistic threat. He contends that without such acknowledgment only superficial progress can be made. Despite their privileged educational status, the St. Francis students were not naive about racism, poverty, and violence. As we have shown in the chapters on moral responsibility and political processes, however, students were not paralyzed by the challenges that they face. Rather, many expressed a sense of agency and responsibility to be forces for social change. We argue that this activism comes from an ability to feel that one is part of a historical tradition that has moral authority.

Conclusion

This chapter has examined the interrelations between students' participation in the community-service program and their understanding of being a Black American. We have argued that serving at the soup kitchen and participating in the social justice class may help an activist sense of identity emerge in three ways. First, experiences at the soup kitchen not only lend clarity to the extent and depth of social problems, but they also illustrate how students can participate in turning bad situations around. The experience of being appreciated for helping another may be particularly powerful for Black adolescents who believe that they are regarded with suspicion by strangers. Second, the social justice curriculum bolstered the sense that change is possible by offering examples of moral triumph and inviting students to become part of an 18-year tradition of service at St. Francis.

Third, service experience and the course helped students to define the moral imperative of confronting social problems such as poverty, discrimination, and violence. While contemporary society has closely linked race to each of these issues, students had historical knowledge and knew that social problems transcend race. They are human problems, and in combating them, students fight to create a more inclusive society.

For many students, service and the course can be thought of as an *encounter* that stirred students to evaluate their identity as Black Americans. It encouraged them to reflect on the present condition of Black America and their role in enacting positive change for the future. In chapter 8, we report how St. Francis alumni, looking back on their junior-year service several years later, emphasized these two aspects of the experience. They indicate that the awareness, involvement, and hope that service helped inspire were pivotal in guiding their actions and defining their sense of who they would be as adults.

CHAPTER EIGHT

The Continuing Identity Process:
After High School

This chapter presents data that illustrate a further developmental step in the identity process outlined in the preceding chapters. The first part of the chapter shows that some of our students ended the 1993–94 school year with high expectations for continuing to do community service. We demonstrate that the desire to do future service was related to several factors, including the level of reflective thinking expressed in essays, and family and peer volunteering.

A desire to do service in the future may be only youthful enthusiasm, as might be found, say, at the end of summer camp or after a successful school theatrical production. The expressions of feelings in the essays showed that several students derived emotional highs from working at the soup kitchen and having the experience interpreted via the social justice ideology. Even if the promise to serve is ephemeral, however, it may signify an important step in identity development. In any normal life, there must be numerous moments of exhilaration with commitments to action that may or may not be met. The important aspect may be that these provide the individual with landmarks for organizing past experience and provide points of reference that can be returned to when needing to gain one's bearings.

We were fortunate that the school administrators cooperated in helping us solicit alumni to see whether the end-of-year promises to volunteer were mere effusions of enthusiasm or actual predictors of future behavior. In the second part of this chapter, we report on a small sample of alumni we were able to survey and show that there are indeed linkages between signs of a commitment to serve in high school and actual service individuals do years later. We also propose that such data provide evidence for continuity in the identity process, which is fostered by close networks of family and friends. High school commitment cannot be linked simply to adult behavior without taking account of such communities that encourage and shape the direction individuals take in their identity development. In keeping with this idea, we also report on voting behavior, which is a sign of interest in the broader community and signals civic responsibility.

In the third part of this chapter, we describe the identity process in early adult life as expressed in statements written by a subsample of the alumni. We found considerable diversity among the alumni essays, with some retaining the ideological outlook to which they were exposed as juniors, but others taking conscious exception to it. Still others felt tension at not having lived up to the ideals taught in social justice, while another group has stepped away from the ideals but retained the critically reflective attitude the course engendered years ago. The sum of these statements is that junior-year social justice seems to have provided a landmark that these adults still use as a vivid point of reference for making sense of their lives. The social justice class is not just a vague memory but an organizing instrument that gives coherence to the ongoing identity process. While individuals have gone their several ways into adulthood, they maintain continuity with the common ideological past by using it to judge the development they made and the future that lies ahead.

The final section of the chapter is devoted to clarifying the concept of continuity through change. We compare a set of statements made by alumni with the essays they wrote as high school juniors to show thematic linkages across time.

Projected Volunteering, 1993–94

At the end of the 1993–94 school year, students were asked on a five-category Likert scale how likely they were to do volunteer service in the upcoming summer (short term) or during college and after education is complete (long term). Not surprisingly, the majority of students responded positively that they were "somewhat" or "very likely" to volunteer in the short term (61%) and the long term (63%). A smaller proportion of students indicated that they would "definitely" volunteer in the short term (19%) and the long term (19%). To determine which factors differentiated students who were definite about volunteering from those who were not, we performed a series of analyses on the data described in table 8.1. Column 1 reports short- and long-term projections according to whether students *had previously participated regularly in volunteer service* beyond working at the soup kitchen as part of the social justice course. Few students not doing extra service said they would definitely volunteer this summer (12%),

Table 8.1 Predictors of Short- and Long-Term Projections
of Volunteering (percentages)

	Self		Family		Friends		Reflective Level	
	No	Yes	No	Yes	No	Yes	No	Yes
Definitely volunteer								
Short term								
No	88	73*	87	71*	85	64*	84	76
Yes	12	27	13	29	15	36	16	23
Long term								
No	86	81	90	75*	90	68*	91	74*
Yes	14	19	10	25	10	32	9	26

Notes. Sample sizes reflect number of students who completed at least two essays and provided information about community service on their questionnaires. N is 111, except for Reflective Level, when N is 114.
*Spearman's r_s, $p < .05$.

while more students already doing service said they were likely to volunteer this summer (27%). This result was not repeated for long-term projections of service.

Column 2 reports projections according to whether *family members participated regularly in volunteer service*. Only 13% of students whose family members were not doing service said they would volunteer this summer versus 29% whose family members were doing service. A comparable result was obtained for long-term projections; only 10% of the students whose family did not do service, but 25% whose family did service, said they were likely to volunteer in the future.

Column 3 reports short- and long-term projections according to whether *friends participated regularly in volunteer service*. For both projections, results were statistically significant. Only 15% of students without friends in service, but 36% with friends in service, said they would volunteer in the summer. Comparable data for long-term projections were 10% for students whose friends did not participate, and 32% whose friends did service.

Column 4 presents projections according to whether students made *reflective statements on their final soup-kitchen essay*. Only long-term projections were significant, as 9% of the students without a reflective statement said they would volunteer in the future, while 26% of the students with reflective statements said they would volunteer in the future.

The best predictor of whether students imagine themselves volunteering in the future is located in their immediate network of family and friends. Reflection on their own service experience during the past year also contributes to projected service. This combination of findings helps to reinforce what we demonstrated in the previous chapters, that the public and personal sides of the service experience are closely intertwined. Taking a reflective stance on service and living in a network in which members do service are two sides of one coin.

We now turn to the alumni data to add more information to our evolving picture of the identity process. One question to be answered is whether effects of this social justice class persist into early adult life. In looking at alumni who took this class up to 11 years ago, is there evidence for a lasting ideological outlook and ethic of personal responsibility of the social justice class? And is it still the case that individuals in networks with the ethos of volunteering are themselves likely to have volunteered as adults?

A Study of 121 Alumni

Three classes of graduates from this high school were contacted through addresses in the alumni records kept by the school. Attempts to contact alumni were made in the winter of 1994 with the graduating classes of 1992, 1990, and 1985, the last being the oldest class that was demographically similar to our 1993–94 juniors. Of a total of 462 questionnaires we mailed, 51 were returned completed by alumni, 20 were returned by the postal service for incorrect addressees, and 391 were not returned. We sent reminder postcards to the addresses in the last category three weeks after the first mailing. After a period of another month, we attempted to contact by phone all the individuals from whom we had not yet received replies. The school administration was able to provide telephone numbers for 300 students who had not responded. We tried to reach these alumni for a 20-minute telephone interview covering many of the items on the written questionnaire. We were successful in 96 cases, producing a combined sample of questionnaires and telephone interviews of 147 alumni comprising 61 graduates from 1992, 60 graduates from 1990, and 26 graduates from 1985.

These totals represented 50%, 36%, and 43% of the alumni for whom we had addresses and phone numbers in the three respective classes. The final sample size for graduates from 1990 was reduced to 34 because 26 female graduates who responded had not taken social justice or worked at the soup kitchen. These alumnae had started at St. Francis in their senior year as part of the transitional period when the school became coeducational. Thus, the final alumni sample totaled 121.

The characteristics of the 121 alumni were as follows: 76% were males and 24% were females; this ratio is explainable by the fact that the school began to admit females only in 1989. There were no females in the 1985 sample, 5 females came from the class of 1990, and 24 females came from the class of 1992. Eighty-nine percent of alumni were Black and 11% were not. Eighty-five percent of alumni had either graduated from or presently were enrolled in college. Of the 36 alumni not currently enrolled in school, 78% worked full-time, 6% worked part-time, 10% did not work, and 6% did not provide employment information. Regarding religious affiliation, 85% of alumni said they were currently affiliated with a religious denomination; 48% were Catholic, 26% were Baptist, 13% were other Protestant, and 13% specified other or no religious affiliation. Fifty-five percent of alumni attended religious services on a weekly or monthly basis. With the exception of gender, the alumni characteristics correspond roughly to the school's current composition. We were not surprised to find that the 1993–94 class has a slightly higher percentage of Black, non-Catholic students, because educational researchers have reported this trend in the composition of inner-city parochial schools (e.g., Bryk, Lee, and Holland 1993).

Our first interest was determining whether alumni had done volunteer service either during high school, at any time after high school graduation, or at present. Forty-four percent said they had done service voluntarily while they were in high school; this service was beyond that required of their junior-year religion course. Forty-five percent also said they had volunteered sometime since high school graduation, and 32% said they were presently volunteering.

We next asked whether having done volunteer service while in high school was predictive of having done volunteer service after high school graduation. Table 8.2 displays the data pertaining to this question. Of the 68 alumni who had not done volunteer service during high school, 29% had volunteered after high school. Of the 51 alumni who volunteered during high school, 68% had volunteered after graduation. Ac-

Table 8.2 Relationships between Measures of Civic Involvement in 121 Alumni
from the Classees of 1992, 1990, and 1985 (percentages)

	Service during high school (N = 119)**			Service during high school (N = 120)*	
	No	Yes		No	Yes
Service since graduation			Service today		
No	71	32	No	76	58
Yes	29	68	Yes	24	42

	Service today (N = 119)**			Service today (N = 119)**	
	No	Yes		No	Yes
Family service			Peer service		
No	67	37	No	56	29
Yes	33	63	Yes	44	71

Note. Sample sizes are less than 121 because a few alumni did not answer all questions
on the questionnaire.
*Chi-square, $p < .075$.
**Chi-square, $p < .05$.

cording to a chi-square test, volunteering after high school graduation
was statistically predicted by having volunteered during high school.

The right-top portion of table 8.2 shows the relationship between
having volunteered during high school and doing volunteer service
today. Of the 68 alumni who had not volunteered during high school,
24% were volunteering at present. Of the 52 alumni who said they had
volunteered during high school, 42% were doing volunteer service at
present. The relation between high school and present volunteering
was dampened by the most recent (1992) graduates, of whom only 15
of 61 volunteered at present. As will be seen from the alumni essays,
many 1992 alumni reported that they were struggling with personal
problems and the chore of completing their college education. Many
felt they should be doing service and hoped that after graduation they
would be able to devote time to this endeavor.

While it is obvious that doing service in high school does not determine volunteer service after graduation; the relations just described indicate continuity across time in individuals. A greater proportion of alumni who did not do volunteer service in high school, versus those who did serve, tended not to volunteer in the years after graduation—71% versus 32%. In complement, a greater proportion of those who served voluntarily during high school, versus those who did not serve, continued to do service in the years following after graduation—68% versus 29%. This finding is congruent with McAdam's (1988) and Fendrich's (1993) reports that active involvement in the civil rights effort predicted continued involvement in the political process years later.

A related question pertained to the process that might help mediate continued service. We therefore assessed whether having family members or friends who did volunteer service was related to continued service. The relationship between one's own present volunteering and family volunteering is shown in the lower-left part of table 8.2. Of the 81 alumni who did not volunteer at present, 33% had family members who were volunteering. Of the 38 alumni who were presently volunteering, 63% had other family members who were also presently volunteering. A comparable result was obtained for the relationship between present volunteering and having friends who volunteer. Of the 81 alumni who were not presently volunteering, 44% had friends who presently volunteered. Of the 38 who were volunteering at present, 71% had friends who were also volunteering.

These results help to specify at least part of the process that mediates continued service. One's close communities of families and friends help create an ethos that supports service and provides opportunities for service. This was found in our 1993–94 sample with respect to projected volunteering (see table 8.1) and has been reported for a national sample of high school students (Hodgkinson and Weitzman 1990) who said they learned about service opportunities from family and friends. Previous research on civil rights activists, crisis-center volunteers, and inner-city adolescents engaged in extensive service activities also support the conclusion that family relationships can play an important role in encouraging service participation (Clary and Miller 1986; Hart and Fegley 1995; Rosenhan 1970). Complementary research on the role of peers was not found in the literature, indicating a neglected area of study.

In keeping with findings reported by McAdam and Fendrich, we wanted to determine whether present service was part of a larger syndrome that included other signs of civic involvement. For this purpose, we asked alumni whether they had voted in the most recent national or local elections of 1992. We were unable to perform a statistical test because almost all the alumni from 1990 and 1985 had voted, leaving insufficient variation in the sample. Of the 60 alumni from the 1990 and 1985 classes, 87% said they had voted in the national and 77% said they had voted in the local 1992 elections. These high rates correspond to those reported by Fendrich (1993) for his college-educated Black sample, whom he termed "ideal citizens." These rates of voting are higher than one finds in the general population or among Black citizens at large. In the 1992 presidential election, 39% of 18- to 20-year-olds and 46% of 21- to 24-year-olds reported voting. Among the Black voting-age population, 54% reported voting in 1992 (U.S. Department of Commerce 1994).

We do not intimate that this sign of civic involvement can be traced to the high school service experience. Rather, we suggest that the alumni's current civic involvement measured through service and voting probably reflects individuals' orientations to society of which the high school experience is a major part. Other aspects include the families, which had chosen to send these alumni to this high school, indicating greater than average interest in their academic achievement and value orientation to life. Indeed, family influence is still a potent factor affecting present volunteering. Another part of this large picture includes friends, whose own volunteering is predictive of the alumni's present volunteering.

Alumni Essays

Of the 51 surveys that were returned by mail, 46 contained essays in which alumni responded to a probe written by Mr. Siwek: "Now that your time at high school and the soup kitchen are some years distant, please take a few moments to write a short essay reflecting upon the relationship between the values and ideas which you learned in junior religion, and the person you are today. Was a measurable, lasting impact made upon you in class and at the kitchen? In what ways? Or have the values and experience faded?"

Twenty-two essays were written by the 1992 graduates, most of whom were now in college, 12 essays were received from 1990 graduates, and 12 essays were received from the 1985 graduates, who were now 11 years beyond their junior-year religion course.

We identified eight themes that we considered continuations of ideas spawned in the junior-year course in social justice. (1) Some alumni said that social justice had awakened them to problems in society and opened them to the plight of people such as the homeless. (2) About an equal number of alumni said that this course and its service component brought them into contact with people who were different, people they might otherwise not have known about. The specific descriptions fit the formal concept of discovery of the *other,* denoting the realization that persons known through stereotypes become on contact more individualized and human (Jahoda 1992).

(3) Several alumni said that the course had been valuable in conveying their responsibility to help others less fortunate than they, but that at present, they were too busy and immersed in personal problems to serve others. (4) In a variant of this theme, other alumni expressed guilt at not being able to serve at present; however, they promised to do service later once their personal problems were put behind them.

(5) Some alumni said they had retained the ideological perspective that was explicitly taught in the course; their essays repeated ideas found in the essays written by the 1993–94 students, which are excerpted in prior chapters. (6) An equal number of alumni repeated these ideas but said that they now thought differently and disagreed with their junior-year views. (7) In a variant of this position, alumni who noted a change in viewpoint added a tinge of cynicism toward the idea that one person can make a difference in the world. (8) A further distinction was made by some alumni who pointed out that the social justice course had taught them how to think critically and that this formed the basis for their current ability to reflect on society and judge it politically and morally.

Each of these themes appeared in at least three essays, and some essays articulated more than one theme. In presenting examples of these themes, we note how they fit our model of the identity process. We view service as a means for promoting reflection on one's place in society's political and moral traditions. Awareness of problems in society is a crucial step in asking how society is organized and how its present structure came into being or ought to be changed. A related insight is that there exist others who share my taken-for-granted humanity, but who differ from me and typically remain outside my frame of reference.

Awareness. "I am glad I did go to the soup kitchen in my junior year in school . . . It made me realize [what] life really is. One day you can be the richest person and then one day you can lose it all" (1992/303[Male]).

"Social Justice class definitely changed me for the better. I used to argue constantly with Mr. Siwek about issues such as homelessness, gun control, defense spending, etc. Those arguments served to give me a new sense of responsibility and awareness. That class changed me from a 'smart kid with a future' to a 'smart kid with a future who gived a damn' " (1990/213[M]).

"The values and ideas I learned in junior religion were that there were a lot of problems in the world like homelessness, nuclear arms, the poor and violence" (1985/107[M]).

Discovery of the other. "Mr. Siwek's class taught to me to think about more than myself. It taught me to take a look outside and to realize all the less fortunate people in the world. I used to complain about how little *I thought* I had, until I saw people standing and lying in the street with less" (1992/320[Female]).

"Working at [the soup kitchen] taught me there are people who are less fortunate than me. Before going there, I always thought of homeless people as being dumb, uneducated, dirty individuals. After meeting with some of them, I realized that most of them did not want to be homeless or come to a soup kitchen. Most of them I talked with were college graduates, young mothers, and everyday people just like everybody else" (1992/327[F]).

"I really got to see how the other half lives—the unfortunate ones. When I used to see a person on the street panhandling, I would ignore them. Now I see that even poverty stricken, they are people too" (1985/108[M]).

The next two themes refer specifically to agency and the course's emphasis on the responsibility to take action to correct societal problems. Insofar as students incorporated this kind of agency into their emerging identity, any present noninvolvement or inactivity may evoke tension or guilt and the soft promise to become involved again at some indefinite later date.

Involvement in personal problems, promise to help later. "The values and ideas I learned in Junior religion class are still in me, but I do not have the time for a lot of extra activity. I am in school trying to help myself and I cannot help others if I cannot help myself. I am too busy to be worrying about other people and things. I am worried about myself because if I don't, I may be homeless one day. Once I finish my plans for the future, I would not mind helping others" (1992/311[F]).

"Although I am not as active with community service as I was at St. Francis, not a day goes by that I don't think about the homeless. However, I just don't have the time to do so. Hopefully after school I will" (1990/209[M]).

"I was politically active in college on issues ranging from Central America, South Africa, the CIA, a multi cultural society, etc. Mr. Siwek's class opened my eyes on the plight of the homeless along with many other issues. These values remain, although submerged under the pressures of daily life" (1985/104[M]).

Guilt at not helping, but wanting to serve. "I want to participate in helping the homeless again as soon as possible. It is something that I have got to do for myself and something I ought to do for Mr. Siwek. In religion class he named me 'Speaks from his heart,' but I haven't been. Now I have to start giving from the heart again so I can feel the sense of love and appreciation for those less fortunate" (1992/309[M]).

"Now I am a sophomore in college. I am not currently as active in the community as I used to be. My goal is to get myself together (i.e., academically, job-wise, spiritually) before I return home to help others. This seems to be a little selfish, but I want to empower myself with as many resources as possible now and then I will have a means to operate by when I return home to my community. At that time I will accept due responsibility as a member of and for my community" (1992/323[F]).

"I've thought a lot about getting up at 7 and hopping on the Metro to [Stop X] and banging on the back door [of the soup kitchen]. I don't know what's kept me from doing it. Maybe when I graduate and head back home, I'll pay them a visit" (1990/203[M]).

The last four themes signify the ongoingness of the identity process. It is not the case that identity is "achieved" on completion of high school or that the effect of the social justice course is the internalization of particular ideals that were espoused. Rather, the value of such a course is that it can stimulate critical reflection, which is needed as youth decide which traditions and ideologies can support their identities that are in the making. We find that some alumni have continued to think along the same ideological lines they did as high school juniors, while other alumni have altered their thinking to arrive at an opposite political pole. Still others have shed their idealism in favor of more realistic or even cynical outlooks. All these positions are encompassed in the theme of critical thinking; alumni note that the course jarred them out of passive acceptance of society as it is and started them on a path of critical thinking about society and what it might be. This questioning is still in progress.

Retention of the class's "liberal" perspective. "I am currently working (volunteer) to help the homeless find jobs and homes. My life long aspiration is to be able to start a program where all homeless can be helped in some way. My expectation is that if this program can catch on and a bill—like the health bill—is passed, we can eliminate this plague" (1992/322[F]).

"Right now I have the world in my hand. I am three months from a Harvard degree. I will be attending either Harvard or Yale law school in fall. I am almost guaranteed more money, success, and material goods than any Black kid from northeast DC could ever imagine. However, I plan to dedicate myself to creating the same opportunities for other kids in the inner city that I had. Social Justice class did this. The impact of that class was immeasurable" (1990/213[M]).

Changed viewpoints. "I am not the same person now that I was before the junior year and I don't think anyone leaves [Mr. Siwek's] class unchanged. While I don't agree with a lot of Mr. Siwek's views and beliefs, I am a lot more aware and educated about many social ills which plague our society" (1992/328[F]).

"The Gun Control laws especially interested me when I was in school. At that time I thought to myself that I could do something, write a letter or something. I now know that if you want something done it takes money. Kennedy said something along the lines of 'Radical change takes radical action.' Well I say, 'Radical change takes radical money'" (1990/208[M]).

"Politics and current events remain my main intellectual hobbies. While still a 'leftist,' I believe my essays of 1984 reflect a 'liberal bigotry' that I tell myself I can't feel today. My main value in this area at present seems to be that informed choice on which stance to take on social or political issues is the key—not some blind adherence to one ideology or another . . . With the cold war over, however, I am much less a dove.

Mr. Siwek and I would probably disagree about such issues as Bosnia, etc. today" (1985/109[M]).

Changed views, cynicism. "Of course, I feel for those people who are in need but it seems that whatever I have done or will do will not put a dent in hunger/homelessness . . . That's just the way the world is it seems. You have to have the rich in order to have the poor, you have the dead with the living, etc. It's the natural order of things" (1992/310[M]).

"The person I am today is somewhat the same in that I still realize we have problems like homelessness, poverty, guns, violence and international differences, only today the problems in society are on a much larger scale. Also, I am a much different person in that I don't believe one person can make a difference or group of people banded together. I . . . [have] come to the conclusion that there is no hope for the world, it is only going to get worse . . . I will never forget the images I saw in class, the kitchen, or on the streets of Washington, New York, or any other place I visit, of people needing help. But I always ask myself for the little that I can help, what difference does it make?" (1985/107[M]).

Established and ongoing critical thinking. "Mr. Siwek provided something for me that I am extremely grateful and thankful for. It is the ability to think or attempt to think critically" (1992/307[M]).

"Our most vivid memories were of that class and the soup kitchen. Of course we didn't like getting up early and oftentimes we made fun of the people who came there. But, in retrospect, I can think of few things that stick in my mind more than that soup kitchen. My family has always been very liberal so Social Justice wasn't really a shock to my system. But I learned to look at the world in a completely different light. Always question authority. [A guest speaker] taught us to question the *status quo*" (1990/203[M]).

"Mr. Siwek's class and the associated community service was fundamental in building the base on which my current views now rest. I attended a Quaker college and ended up doing two years in the Peace Corps. I'd say that St. Francis and the intellectual climate it produced were instrumental in guiding me in those decisions" (1985/109[M]).

"Visiting the soup kitchen and going through Mr. Siwek's class represent a phase in my life in which I made a transformation. I was on the brink of becoming one of those hoodlums the world so fears. This class was one of the major factors in choosing the right path. I saw people in the soup kitchen. I talked with them. They were regular people who had been spit out by society. I wanted to know what led to these conditions. Being a Black man, I was concerned first by the plight of Black people. Mr. Siwek's class and the soup kitchen experience started my search for these deeper truths" (1985/112[M]).

These excerpts illustrate the overarching point that, even as individuals move beyond adolescence into adult life, they maintain continuity with their past. Our data, of course, are biased to produce continuity because alumni were told to focus explicitly on their junior-year experience in social justice. However, we are not arguing that continuity is manifested in internalization of the material acquired in the junior year. Instead, we propose that what lasted from this course was a clear landmark from which further reflection on society, confrontation of ideological understandings of society, and plans for active support of these outlooks could be judged.

The essays illustrate that alumni were able to connect their present stances back to the social justice experience. For those too busy to think directly about service, reference to the course prodded recall of how it made them aware of social ills by confronting them with the reality of homelessness. For others, who still do service, the course brought out capacities they might otherwise not have known they possessed. For still other alumni, the course was vivid, but they have deviated from it by adopting different views on society and ways to address its problems. This diversity makes sense, since alumni have left the uniform experiences of the high school and taken individual paths toward adulthood. Despite these changes, alumni were able to connect their current positions coherently with their past experience so that their current self-perceptions were linked to this landmark experience in the junior year.

This argument concurs with McAdam's analysis (1988) of continuity in personal narratives that bear individuals' identity. It is also supported by the quantitative data reported in the previous section of this chapter. Individuals who volunteered beyond the requirements of the social justice class are still distinguished by their likelihood to do volunteer service. Moreover, individuals who do service live in networks in which family members and friends also do volunteer service. This active stance toward correcting society's ills is abetted by the political conviction of voting, thus forming a syndrome of democratic activism. We cannot identify all the roots, which are probably widespread, but the junior-year experience seems to be an important and obvious source from which the identity process took its direction and around which it can continue to develop in a coherent manner.

Continuity and Change from High School to Early Adulthood

In this final section of the chapter, we illustrate the forgoing points by comparing statements written by alumni in 1994 with essays the same individuals wrote when they were in the social justice class four to six years earlier. Mr. Siwek had saved soup-kitchen essays written by the classes of 1990 and 1992, but did not have essays for the class of 1985. We focus on three points of continuity—an empathic outlook toward the other, reflectivity on the self's agency, and relating one's own agency to helping less fortunate individuals.

Empathy toward the Other

Respondent 327 is a Black alumna who graduated in 1992 and is currently enrolled in college. She is politically moderate, votes, reads news magazines, and regularly discusses political issues with family members but not with friends. She has not done volunteer service since high school.

In October 1990, she wrote: "One homeless woman came to me and said, 'You look just like my daughter, black and pretty.' I said, 'Thank you.' I asked her where her daughter was and she told me she didn't know. She just hoped her daughter was making something of herself [more] than she did. Right then and there, she began to cry. I told her don't worry and that her daughter will be alright."

In the spring of 1994, when asked to describe the impact of the social justice class, the same female wrote: "Mr. Siwek's class has had a lasting impact on me. His class taught me that there are people suffering much more than we as a society may think and it is time for a change. I feel that my view about certain things has not changed since my junior year, only my life [has changed]."

Respondent 322 is also a Black female presently enrolled in college. She is a political moderate, votes, reads news magazines, and discusses political issues with her family and friends. She has continued to do volunteer service and volunteers at a shelter for the homeless in the city where she attends college. In October 1990, she wrote: "My best moment was when this elderly man told me 'Thank you; thank you for this food. Thank you for serving this to me. God bless you.' I never had such a wonderful feeling . . . [Another] man made me laugh. He came through the line and I said, 'Would you like a peanut butter sandwich?' He told me 'Quite frankly, no. There is no way you can make me eat that sandwich.' Then he smiled."

In the spring 1994, the same female wrote: "I am currently working (volunteer) to help the homeless find jobs and homes. My life long aspiration is to be able to start a program where all homeless can be helped in some way. My expectation is that if this program can catch on and a bill—like the health bill—is passed, we can eliminate this plague. *No one* should be without, if we are truly a 'land of milk and honey.' "

Ongoing Self-Reflection

Respondent 328 is a Black female presently in an elite college for Black females and is majoring in mathematics. She is somewhat active politically and volunteers in a legal clinic in the city where she attends college. This is what she wrote in October 1990: "I found myself questioning myself about what I would do if I were in the predicament that these people were in. At that moment I became very disappointed with myself because I realized that I was a very selfish person. These people live day to day wondering—Will I eat?, while I live day to day wondering—What do I want to eat?"

In the spring of 1994, the same female wrote: "As a result of my experience [in the junior year], I am much more compassionate towards people, more tolerant of homosexuality, and simply *better educated*. I think that the most meaningful thing this class does is . . . force you to think about important issues and to evaluate yourself and what you're made of."

Respondent 206 is a Black male still in college. He is a political moderate, votes, reads news magazines, discusses politics rarely, and has not volunteered since high school. In October 1988, he wrote: "Here I am in the soup kitchen putting potatoes and green peppers down the shredder . . . and picking tiny bits of left over chicken off the bones. I thought to myself how disgusting this was and is this what people eat."

In 1994, he wrote: "Yes, my experience at the kitchen has made a lasting impact. I still remember those rotten potatoes and tomatoes. It makes me sick."

Later in his 1988 essay, he wrote: "After looking at . . . their faces I kind of felt what they were going through. I saw embarrassment in the faces and the innocence in their eyes. I really felt like grabbing a bowl of soup and going out in the cafe, sit at a table filled with the worst men and talk to them because no one should have to suffer like they do."

Later in his 1994 statement he wrote: "Today I am more reluctant to give a homeless person money. Not because I am mean or scared but simply because I am struggling myself for money. I know it seems selfish and it actually is. However, it is just the way I have developed."

Using One's Agency to Assist Others in Need

Respondent 321 is a Black female college student majoring in business. She is politically moderate and uninvolved in politics. She volunteers at a hospital once a week and has done this for two years. In October 1990, she wrote: "[The soup-kitchen workers] were telling us that the homeless [are] just like us but their luck just ran out, that's all. When I was stirring the soup and making salads and sandwiches, something got to me. I was thinking, it could be me or you one day, you never know what the future may hold for us. Your health may go bad, your company go bankrupt or something."

In 1994, she wrote: "I am glad I did go to the soup kitchen in my junior year. The reason is because it made me realize [how] life really is. One day you can be the richest person there is and then one day you can lose it all."

Later in her 1990 essay, she wrote: "[The best moment of the day] was when I served food to them and they said thank you so much and may God bless you. It made me think how grateful I am to have somebody to care for me and they don't have [anybody] to love and care for them each and every day."

In parallel in her 1994 essay, she wrote: "I still think about the times I have gone to the soup kitchen and fed them. It made me feel good to see another happy face that I made feel good for that day. Maybe one of these days the country might see to it that everybody can have a place to stay."

Respondent 213 is the Black male Harvard undergraduate quoted earlier in the chapter who had been accepted to law school at Harvard and Yale. He is a member of several clubs, politically active, votes, and has done volunteer service since high school. In October 1988, he wrote: "The soup and the sandwiches became thin and were running out, and a man asked me for two sandwiches. I thought how could he be so selfish when he has 50 people in line behind him. Then I came to the conclusion that he was not selfish, the American people were selfish, and as a result, he was out on the street."

In 1994, three months before his college graduation, he wrote: "That class changed me from a 'smart kid with a future' to a 'smart kid with a future who gived a damn.' I have always been a nice and caring person but I didn't see things the way I do now until 11th grade religion."

Later in his 1988 essay, he wrote: "The kitchen was not horrible as my classmates had told me. The only horrible thing was a mother and two year old daughter in the line. I didn't think about it for real until the little girl came to the window, stretched out her hand and asked, 'Can I have one more sandwich, please?' I felt like giving her 100 sandwiches, not only 100 sandwiches but a house and her mother a job. When she walked away with the peanut butter sandwich, I could only ask myself, 'Why?'"

At the end of his 1994 essay, he wrote: "I have the world in my hand. I am three months from a Harvard degree. I will be attending either Harvard or Yale law school in fall. I am almost guaranteed more money, success, and material goods than any Black kid from northeast DC could ever imagine. However, I plan to dedicate myself to creating the same opportunities for other kids in the inner city."

Conclusion

Three findings stand out from this array of results. First, the social justice class was a landmark in the memory of these young adults as they were constructing their adult identities. For some, the junior year marked a moment of awakening to the reality of social problems in this land of plenty. The experience of meeting and serving homeless persons roused sensitivity to poverty, the distribution of wealth, the humanity underneath the dirtiness of homelessness, and the possibility within these alumni to be part of the solution instead of passive observers to society's problems. Even when alumni were not now volunteering or disagreed with the ideology espoused in social justice, the message was recalled vividly either to pique their conscience or to serve as a point from which they have consciously departed.

Second, the youthful promise to volunteer, perhaps engendered in a moment of junior-year exhilaration, may have been more than that. Students who thought they might volunteer lived predominantly in social surrounds where family members and friends were actual volunteers. In fact, having a social network in which there is an ethos of volunteering was a key factor associated with alumni's volunteering. The identity process is as much driven by social interaction and the public exchange of reflections as it is pushed ahead through private thinking. The synergy between essays and group discussions in previous chapters supported this conclusion. And the contingency results from tables 8.1 and 8.2 show in a new way that building volunteer service into one's identity is a personal as well as a socially constructed process.

Third, we propose that the various excerpts from alumni help illustrate the meaning of continuity in the identity process. When asked to use social justice class as a point of reference, these young adults could judge themselves clearly as having maintained or deviated from the ideology that emphasized the individual's responsibility to confront and help correct society's problems. Several alumni stated that their lives had changed due to meeting new challenges, such as getting through the rigors of college or battling with financial difficulties. Having adapted to these conditions, the alumni still viewed themselves as continuing on the same path toward identity that originated during the awakening of the social justice experience.

We underline the third point with an example from an alumnus, 212, still in college. In 1988, he had written of his day at the soup kitchen in the metaphorical language of a Halloween party. The workers came in costume and so did the homeless, in their costumes of the streets. The homeless came to the kitchen door for tricks or treats; some were in ill humor, but others were polite and pleased with the festivities. At the end of his essay, he said: "They keep coming and the food keeps going. We run out but they don't. The party's over—for them."

Six years later this alumnus wrote: "I do not know what a preposition is. I do not remember who the eighth President of the United States was. I do not remember how to find the angle of an obtuse triangle. All these things from high school I cannot recall. What I remember is [watching on the television monitor in class] the image of an old trembling woman . . . standing at her doorway with one hand cupped, with the other hand making an upward motion to her mouth. She is too embarrassed by the television camera to ask the volunteer worker to bring food next time, so she makes the motion. Was a lasting impact made upon me . . . ? I do not pass a homeless person without emptying my pockets. I do not stay silent when someone starts making fun of gays. I make sure to vote when a measure of gun control comes up . . . I don't know where my Chemistry 101 book is but my social justice book is still on my shelf."

CHAPTER NINE

Ten Ideas for Designing and Implementing Community-Service Programs

During the past decade, an extensive educational literature has accumulated on community-service programs. A large portion is devoted to curriculum and programmatic features that enhance service effectiveness. Service learning, which denotes an educational method integrating community service into an academic curriculum, has gained increased prominence. One of our goals in writing this book was to offer insight into the design and implementation of service-learning programs.

We outline ten ideas that educators and programmers may find helpful. We base our conclusions on our case study of the St. Francis service program, supplemented by our review of the empirical literature on service by adolescents. The literature review (Yates and Youniss 1996b) covers 44 studies and includes investigations of the characteristics and motivations of service participants, the day-to-day experience of service, and the outcomes of service participation. Although the St. Francis data come from a school-based program, the ideas are applicable to community-based programs.

The ten ideas reflect our major thesis that service can provide concrete opportunities for youth to develop an increased understanding of their membership within a societal framework and their responsibility for society's future. In order for service to have such a profound influence on youth's identity, it cannot be presented to youth as an isolated experience. Rather, it needs to become integrated in their lives. With this goal, the ten ideas place particular emphasis on the form of service activity, supporting curriculum, and people with whom youth serve.

Some of these ideas are extensions of issues that have been identified by service advocates. For example, the Corporation for National and Community Service (1994) and the Alliance for Service-Learning in Education Reform (1993) have issued statements regarding standards for high-quality service programs. These statements specify that service activities should address real needs and that service programs should enhance connections in the community. They also emphasize that participants and staff should understand the mission and goals of service and that youth should have opportunities for reflection after their participation. In this chapter, we elaborate upon these standards and illustrate how they are relevant to the St. Francis program. We also bring up other ideas that have not been frequently discussed, but that appear pivotal to the St. Francis program. These ideas include having participants work as a group, acknowledging the diversity of participants' experiences, and framing service as a history-making process. All ten ideas touch upon the common themes of engaging youth in society and making service an integral part of their identity.

1. Meaningful Activity

In assessing community-service programs, questions about the frequency and length of service often arise. The St. Francis study supports the notion that quality of service is more important than quantity. Students at St. Francis were required to serve at the soup kitchen for a relatively short period, on four occasions for approximately 20 hours. Yet ten years later, their experience at the kitchen remained a landmark event that alumni believed shaped who they were in high school and who they are today.

What qualities of a service activity help to make it meaningful to an individual's sense of identity? In *Principles for High Quality Service Programs* (1994), the Corporation for National and Community Service emphasizes that service activities should address real needs and consider the unique qualities, including age, of participants. Newmann and Rutter's description (1983, 2) of "developmental opportunities" further contributes to defining meaningful service activities by identifying features such as "having responsibility to make decisions, identifying and reflecting upon one's personal values, working closely with adults, facing new and challenging situations, and receiving appropriate blame or credit for one's work done."

Preparing and serving meals at a soup kitchen as part of an organized program provides these types of opportunities, as do activities such as child care, hospital work, mentoring, renovating buildings, and cleaning parks. We add to Newmann and Rutter's list one further quality of service that was central to the St. Francis students' experience and that may make some service activities more beneficial than others. In written essays and discussion groups, students focused on the profound impact of interacting with people who have been stereotyped and marginalized by society. These encounters forced many students to reflect on the conflict between their preconceptions about homeless people and the reality of individuals who urgently needed help. Often when students articulated a sense of commitment to service in the future, they framed it in terms of having been motivated by a homeless person they had met.

This motivation did not take the form of pity or charity, but rather of respect for another person and moral indignation at present social conditions. For example, student 603, who was quoted in chapter 4, described in her final essay an encounter with a homeless man that led her to reflect on how she should respond to him: "There was a man [at the soup kitchen], I didn't catch his name, but he had an obvious mental problem, and my classmates and I laughed at his actions . . . Then I realized that he was going to be like that forever. There was no one there to help him, and probably no one who cared. It hurt to realize that I was sitting among society's forgotten. The people I read about everyday at school and in newspapers. I wanted to cry, but I didn't, I couldn't, they didn't need my pity. They needed my actions and I didn't know what to do."

The St. Francis students worked hard because they knew that their activities at the soup kitchen were not make-work. The service that they performed engaged them in the urgent problem of poverty in Washington, DC. Students understood that they were performing a vital service by preparing and serving a meal to people who could not afford to buy food and who were often physically ill due to the strains in their lives. They also realized that the brief exchanges and conversations that they had with the people they served were an equally important part of their work. Most students treated the diners with respect and, in this way, offered a form of social interaction that homeless people rarely encounter in their day-to-day lives.

Although there were a few tense exchanges between students and diners over the course of the year, in general students felt that the diners appreciated the care and energy they put into the meal and were grateful for their respectful manner. For many students, this appreciation provided additional motivation to work harder.

The St. Francis findings support prior research in leading to the conclusion that *meaningful activity* (1) addresses a patent social need, (2) challenges youth's ability to organize and take on procedural responsibilities, and (3) encourages youth to engage in social interactions with diverse people. In the St. Francis program, social interactions may have played a particularly vital role in promoting a broadened sense of social relatedness and responsibility.

2. Emphasis on Helping Others

Kahne and Westheimer (1996) offer an analysis of the "politics" of renewed interest in community service in the 1980s and 1990s. They voice concern that much of the rhetoric advocating service is presented within the framework of charity and places inordinate emphasis on personal benefits to the participating youth. They find fault with such goals and especially single out the goal of boosting self-esteem in youth. They argue that charity-oriented service risks promoting "a thousand points of status quo," rather than encouraging caring attitudes toward others and fostering commitment to enact social justice (596).

Emphasizing the personal benefits of service detracts from the unique aspects that distinguish service as a pedagogical experience. Legislation to increase service opportunities specifies both personal and social benefits. For example, the *Senate Report for National Community Service Act of 1990* listed the following benefits: "greater connection to the community, an easier transition from school to work, improved reliability, punctuality, and perseverance, development of self esteem and sense of personal worth, and stronger basic skills and ability to work with others, and critical thinking" (U.S. Senate 1990, 37). By presenting such a laundry list of benefits, the distinguishing aspects of this service are lost. Service is not unique in providing the opportunity to improve reliability, punctuality, self-worth, basic skills, and critical thinking. Part-time work or apprenticeship programs can promote the same personal benefits.

What service can uniquely provide for youth are opportunities for growth in moral, social, and civic awareness. In performing meaningful service, youth are asked to engage in activities that probably are not directly connected to their future work aspirations. As the St. Francis students indicated, service has a much broader role. It helped them to understand their lives in relation to others and fostered the sense of being part of a historical process larger than themselves. Service activities sponsored by 4-H clubs and the Boy Scouts provide additional examples of organizations that combine service with worthwhile causes that can capture youth's interests (e.g., Ladewig and Thomas 1987).

When the St. Francis students were asked to recount the "best moment of the day," they frequently focused on a moment when they had helped another individual in less fortunate circumstances. They emphasized that the diners at the kitchen really needed them and that they, in turn, cared about the diners. The act of helping others was what engaged the students. Helping included offering assistance to specific homeless individuals and soup-kitchen staff as well as contributing to solve a social problem. While personal benefits such as heightened self-confidence were undoubtedly derived, emphasis was placed on the *other* more than on the self.

3. Integrated Part of Articulated Ideology

The 1980s and 1990s have witnessed a call for increased service opportunities for youth (Commission on National and Community Service 1993; National Dropout Prevention Network 1992; People for the American Way 1989). Some advocates have proposed making a set number of service hours mandatory for graduation from public high school (Townsend 1992; Wofford 1995). A 1996 survey of the 130 largest public school districts in the United States found that 75% offered service programs, 15% required service districtwide, and 25% of students were affected by these requirements (National and Community Service Coalition 1995). As the momentum for widespread implementation of service programs builds, it is important to be clear about the purpose of service and ways it fits with other life experiences. The worst case would have service become just one more item on a list of requirements to earn a diploma, thus making it one more hurdle to jump and another occasion for cynicism.

The St. Francis program countered cynicism by basing service on religious grounds that were integral to the school's mission. As a parochial school, St. Francis has a mission statement that articulates a definite ideological perspective on education.

> Our mission at St. Francis High School is to teach the message of Christ, to create experience of Christian community and to provide for the liberal education of students from diverse cultural and intellectual backgrounds.
>
> In teaching the message of Jesus, we try to be aware of God's presence which affects all we do.

In creating the experience of community, we value service as a way to respond to God's presence.

In providing academic experience, we seek to challenge the student in ways that make a sense of accomplishment possible.

These experiences at St. Francis nurture the student's spiritual, intellectual, cultural, social, physical and emotional growth.

We do these things in a spirit of mutual support among administrators, faculty, staff, students, parents and alumni, and we encourage an enthusiastic response.

The service program followed from this statement in a coherent way. While this formal mission statement was freely accessible to parents, students, and teachers, it was communicated in more concrete ways through a series of special events held throughout the year. Many of these events were organized by the social justice teachers, who worked hard to extend the experience of serving at the soup kitchen beyond the walls of the religion classroom. One way that this was done was through visual reminders of the school's commitment to serving homeless people. Signs were placed throughout the school; for example, the name of the soup kitchen was painted on the wall of a major corridor, and student posters and collages on homelessness were displayed in the front entrance for one week, twice in the fall and once in the spring. Posters for the Thanksgiving food drive included statements such as "Give from the heart," "Give, nobody wants to be hungry," "Help by giving," and "Feed the hungry as ourselves." Other posters incorporated the name of the school mascot, with statements such as "[St. Francis mascot] means giving," and " St. Francis [mascot] is the food drive." As another visual reminder of the school's connection to the soup kitchen, photographs of students at the soup kitchen were included in the yearbook and in slide shows shown at beginning- and end-of-year assemblies and on parents' night.

Special events also helped to make service at the soup kitchen a pervasive theme. A food drive to fill the soup kitchen's pantry was held at Thanksgiving, and the school sent representatives to participate in a national walkathon for hunger. A field trip was also organized with visits to advocacy organizations such as Amnesty International, Common Cause, and the Peace Corps. Through organizing visual displays and events, the teachers helped make what could be viewed an isolated academic requirement into a defining part of students' high school experience.

The example of St. Francis brings into question whether programs that treat service as just one of many academic requirements can be effective. It challenges programs that are not structured within an explicit ideological framework of, for example, a religious institution or movement-based organization, to articulate clearly the overarching values represented by service participation. This is a particular challenge in the current context of diversity that marks the public educational system.

In her writings on public school reform, Fine (1991) presents one way that service could be understood as part of the general mission of public education. In the conclusion of her study on minority urban dropouts, she offers a vision of the public school system that is community- and advocacy-oriented.

> If this public sphere were dotted with scenes in which multiple voices were heard, then public schools would constitute a splendid site for public conversation. Public sector organizations and social change groups and advocates would be solicited to accept high school interns to witness and participate in activities of social change: tenant organizing, welfare reform, community health care, a newsletter for single parents, investigations into the problems of homelessness, or a study of the complexities and possibilities of a decentralized school district. The point would be to enable young people to experience social problems as mutable, to position themselves as protagonists and makers of social history, to strengthen the sense of community and citizenship that schools intend to nurture, and to create among adolescents their own expertise and knowledge base which would migrate from community to school and back again. (216–17)

Fine describes how in a public school setting, where sides are usually not taken, important social issues can still be addressed by reviewing the several sides that impinge on them. Not stating an opinion does not have to mean that all opinions cannot be articulated and discussed. In a similar fashion to the St. Francis discussion groups, one could imagine encouraging students to voice and debate their opinions so that all views are heard.

For Fine, service is part of a comprehensive plan to reform public education in the United States. It is a piece of a larger puzzle. We believe that, whether a service program is implemented in a private or public school or as part of a community organization, it should be connected to the defining goals of the sponsoring institution. Furthermore, this connection needs to be instantiated not just in a formal mission statement, but also in the daily practices of the sponsoring institution. This recommendation does not mean that all students will or should unquestioningly adopt the ideology. The St. Francis discussion groups show that students debated and struggled to make sense of the ideas with which they were presented in class. The ideology of social justice at St. Francis provided a framework on which, as the alumni showed, students could build as they proceeded toward adulthood.

4. Group Rather Than Individual Action

Another defining characteristic of the St. Francis program was that students performed service as an identifiable group. From the simple fact of arriving at the kitchen at approximately the same time and working together, to being recognized as partaking in an 18-year-old St. Francis tradition, students were able to couple their individual identity with a clear group identity. External supports were provided at the kitchen by signs and gestures that explicitly recognized this tradition. For instance, school bumper stickers were on the wall, and diners and staff members asked casual questions or made comments about the school, the athletic teams, and the social justice class.

Interviews with civil rights participants conducted by McAdam (1988) and Fendrich (1993) support the importance of group awareness. These studies indicate that being part of a group can intensify the short- and long-term commitment of individual participants, even after the group disperses. This argument is further supported by Gamson's findings (1992) that stress how collective action thrives on a clearly defined *we* who act to challenge injustice. By going to the soup kitchen together and being clearly identified as part of the St. Francis tradition of service, students were encouraged to think of themselves as the we who are combating the problems of homelessness.

This idea contradicts the recommendation of some educators and policy makers who state that youth should be given a choice of service activities so that experience is made to match their needs and personal dispositions (Kropp 1994). There is obvious value to recognizing that individuals differ in being suited for particular kinds of tasks. But any advantage from that should be weighed against the additional benefit that comes from having students work together on a common project. The St. Francis students viewed their service at the soup kitchen as part of a common project. They knew that it was part of a tradition at the school that was equivalent to a rite of passage for juniors. Having students come together and share their experiences in discussion groups no doubt reinforced this notion. In the discussion sessions, students talked about junior year being the right time for them to go to the soup kitchen because they believed that they were now mature enough to handle its challenges and to make a contribution. Reflecting the importance of this event, alumni portrayed the soup kitchen and social justice course years later as a defining moment in their high school experience and adolescence.

5. Reflective Opportunities with Peers

Empirical studies strongly support the idea of supplementing service with academic components and reflective opportunities (Cognetta and Sprinthall 1978; Conrad and Hedin 1982; Hamilton and Fenzel 1988; Rutter and Newmann 1989; Schlosberg 1991). Policy advocates have adopted a similar outlook (Corporation for National and Community Service 1994). Participants need to be prepared for their service and have opportunities to be debriefed and reflect on experience afterward. School-based programs often include reflective opportunities in the form of a personal journal and essays such as those required at St. Francis (Newmann and Rutter 1983). The format of written assignments varies, but typically students are required to submit their writings to teachers for feedback in the form of comments rather than grades. It is clear in our data that essays provided a productive way for students to reflect on their experiences. Chapter 4 illustrated that reflective statements became more encompassing over the year as students thought about their service experiences in terms of their own lives and grappled with social realities and theories of justice. Our analysis also indicates that peer discussion groups can have an important pedagogical function. These discussion meetings allowed students to participate in a joint process of thinking through questions stimulated by experiences at the soup kitchen. This public process complemented and extended the reflections in students' private essays. Talking together, students challenged and elaborated on one another's ideas in exchanges that led to consensual validation. (See Youniss and Yates 1996 for further discussion of this point.)

These discussion sessions also reinforced collective membership among students. Students discovered that their peers had similar feelings and ideas about their time at the kitchen, and this realization helped to bolster group cohesion. Students learned that their peers shared their sense of moral indignation about conditions at the soup kitchen and related social issues. They helped each other to define more precisely the sources of their indignation and possible courses of reformative action.

6. Service Organizers as Models and Integrators

People who organize service and work with youth have an important opportunity to educate adolescents through their own example. Although some students at St. Francis disliked Mr. Siwek's demanding and opinionated manner, most expressed respect for him because they believed that he was someone who lived his message. For instance, they knew that for five years Mr. Siwek had lived in a spiritually based community that ran a shelter and a soup kitchen and that for 15 years he had organized the Sunday meal at the soup kitchen. While students learned in their text about other exemplars of service, including public figures, Mr. Siwek was an accessible exemplar with whom they could interact on a daily basis. They learned through him that becoming a teacher was one route to helping others and that even those who care deeply about other people have good and bad days, optimistic and pessimistic moods.

Although we have focused on Mr. Siwek as the organizer of the St. Francis service program, one of the six sections of juniors was taught by Ms O'Connell, who was well qualified to teach social justice. She had been active in service since high school and after college spent time doing volunteer service in Calcutta. Despite these qualifications, as a newcomer to the school, Ms O'Connell had to establish her credibility with the students. In early discussion groups, students expressed regret that they did not have Mr. Siwek. During one discussion group held in December, students talked about how they wanted the excitement of being in Mr. Siwek's class and believed that Ms O'Connell was not demanding respect from her students. As the year progressed, Ms O'Connell became increasingly involved in the school; she organized a weekend club for female students on probation and coached an athletic team. She also volunteered at the soup kitchen on school holidays. These actions reflecting commitment toward the school and community service contributed to the increasing admiration that students expressed toward her as the year progressed.

It seems likely that teachers such as Mr. Siwek and Ms O'Connell play a crucial role in a program's success. Their passion and dedication motivated and unified students. Both teachers were accessible role models of lifetime commitment to service. It seems relevant that alumni's recollections on service at the soup kitchen and the social justice course made frequent reference to how they believed their lives had met or failed to meet the ideals established in Mr. Siwek's class. Although some alumni articulated positions different from Mr. Siwek's, they still judged themselves relative to his criteria, and this finding is suggestive of the lasting impact that dedicated service organizers can have.

7. Site Supervisors as Models

People who work at service sites provide another excellent and underappreciated resource. In the same way as service organizers, they can be models of moral commitment who offer their perspective on social problems and the dynamics of trying to alleviate these problems. While the ability of staff members to be educators may be limited by time and resources, this potential should not be overlooked when service organizers select sites and establish relationships with the staff at these sites.

St. Francis provides a good example of a program in which the people working at the service site took on the role of educators. On numerous occasions, while making sandwiches or cutting vegetables, students talked with kitchen staff about issues such as the increasing number of people coming to eat at the soup kitchen and the gentrification of the soup-kitchen neighborhood. Students also asked staff members about their own lives, how they came to work at the soup kitchen, and why they had chosen a life with little material reward. For example, in her first essay, student 703 gave this account of a conversation with a staff worker.

As I was preparing what seemed like two million sandwiches, I began talking with Jennifer who lives in a house with other people who run the kitchen. I asked her why she wanted to do

that, because she was young. She asked me why I chose to ignore the problems of the poor. I told her I did not choose to
ignore anything, but I was not choosing to devote my life to it.
She understood, she smiled, and that was when I understood
why she directed her life to the poor. As I was serving the soup
and looking into these people's eyes, I was wondering why they
were not saying, "Thank you." Then I realized that they were
so hurt and beaten down that they could not be thankful for
the way I am. They are experiencing a whole other thanks.
The thanks for waking up in the morning, the thanks for not
being arrested, the thanks that they found a bed the night before. The people at the soup kitchen made me realize a new
kind of thanks.

In this way, conversations with staff conducted in the context of
serving homeless individuals encouraged students to reflect seriously
on the connection between their soup-kitchen experience and future
life choices.

Mr. Siwek encouraged the staff's involvement as educators by
maintaining communication during the year, by speaking regularly
with the staff on the phone and visiting the soup kitchen. He also invited the staff to speak at the Thanksgiving and end-of-year assemblies.
To give the staff a better sense of the service program, he sent them
copies of students' essays about the soup kitchen. Staff members told
MY that reading the essays made them feel that they were part of an
important experience for the students and increased their level of support for the program. On receiving the essays, staff members doubled
their efforts to ensure that students were given occasions to interact
directly with the people they served.

The staff also tried to provide opportunities for students to participate in different forms of social activism. These opportunities included
invitations to participate in a demonstration for more affordable housing and to help distribute blankets to people sleeping on the streets.

Essays and discussion groups indicate that students paid attention
to the staff's treatment of the diners and how they ran the soup
kitchen. They were critical of staff members when they were judged to
have acted disrespectfully toward homeless individuals and when the
quality of the food preparation was found wanting. In reflecting on
how the soup kitchen was run, students compared the Monday group,
comprising mainly elderly White female parishioners from an affluent

suburb, to the Tuesday through Friday group, comprising an activist community of White and Black men and women. The students weighed the advantages of the two groups. The Monday group operated with ample financial resources that could buy high-quality food. They established rules of conduct that, most of the time, promoted an orderly atmosphere in the dining room. The Tuesday through Friday group included staff who had been homeless themselves and had known some of the people served for over a decade. Because they lived in the community where the soup kitchen was located, they interacted with many of the people served throughout the day. This group limited the number of rules in the dining room as a way of respecting the individuality of the diners and distinguishing the soup kitchen from other social-service experiences, which can be rule bound. For the most part, students did not dismiss one group and favor the other. Rather, they picked out individuals and organizational practices that they liked and disliked in the two groups.

The example from St. Francis supports Newmann and Rutter's inclusion (1983, 2) of "working closely with adults" as part of their list of developmental opportunities. The Alliance for Service-Learning in Education Reform (1993) also lists skilled adult guidance and supervision as a standard for high-quality service programs. Clearly, the people with whom youth work during their service play a critical role in producing effects in the participants. The St. Francis students benefited from working with several adults who treated them with respect, took an active interest in their involvement, and frankly shared their own experiences of service.

8. Acknowledging Participants' Diversity

The literature on community service describes the importance of planning programs that are developmentally appropriate and build upon individual participants' strengths. For example, in *Principles for High Quality Service Programs* (1994, 4), the Corporation for National and Community Service recommends drawing "on the unique qualities of participants: their abilities, professional education or training, age, diversity, idealism, intelligence, and other assets." We elaborate upon this idea, by pointing out that diversity among participants, service organizers, the staff at the site, and recipients can create potentially uncomfortable situations that require acknowledgment and support.

The literature on community service does not address how the dynamics of race, class, and gender can influence service experience. In the St. Francis program, all of these issues were salient and created a degree of discomfort for participants. In discussion groups, some students indicated conscious awareness that their own minority racial status influenced their experience at a soup kitchen that served a primarily minority population. Students were upset by the large number of young Black men who were in line for food and whom they compared with friends, relatives, and themselves. In trying to understand the situations of the homeless, students sometimes drew upon their own experiences of being prejudged and discriminated against. Showing the pertinence of socioeconomic class as well as race, on several occasions students encountered acquaintances, relatives of friends, and even their own relatives in the food line.

Thus, some students were being asked to volunteer time for people whose economic situations were not far removed from their own. The recognition by students of how close they were to the edge of poverty may have helped them to be more empathic to those they served, but it was painful as well. In fact, some students said that requiring youth who were not economically well off to volunteer for disadvantaged populations was like "throwing it in [their] face," and they argued that service initiatives should focus on middle- and upper-class youth. Adding further complexity to the issue of class, students were often distressed by the preconceptions of homeless people who treated them as if they were rich and spoiled because they went to parochial school.

The issue of gender was important in different ways for the male and female students. For the male students, the activity of preparing and serving food had disturbing gender implications because some felt it was female work. For the female students, tensions sometimes arose because the soup kitchen served a primarily middle-aged male population. It was not uncommon for men to flirt with the female students and pressure them for dates or phone numbers. These young female adolescents were confused about how to respond to such advances. They were concerned about prejudging and hurting the men's feelings but, at the same time, felt the advances were inappropriate and were frightened by them. In one incident, a female student gave her phone number to a man who she subsequently learned from a staff member had attacked two women at a homeless shelter. After learning this, the student did not come to school for a week. She wrote in that quarter's essay that she felt she had acted stupidly and was angry at herself and frightened that the man would contact her.

Like many service programs, the St. Francis program did not supply explicit instructions about ways to handle problems stemming from the dynamics of diversity. While an incident like giving one's phone number to a potentially dangerous man could have been anticipated, it was not. After it occurred, Mr. Siwek told students not to give out their phone numbers, but offered no explanation. Most students articulated the belief that it was common sense not to give one's phone number to a stranger. However, some were confused by the contradiction of being asked to treat individuals at the soup kitchen like a friend or relative but, ultimately, to be wary of them.

The discussion group established by MY provided a forum for students to talk about uncomfortable experiences and to get feedback from their peers. It was within this context that students initiated discussion about the phone-number incident and debated how one should respond to a diner who asked for a date or an address. Through their active participation in these exchanges, students signified that they wanted more opportunities to discuss these types of experiences. The examples from the St. Francis data show that educators and service organizers should not ignore the importance of race, class, and gender in designing programs. They should anticipate their saliency by addressing them so as to turn uncomfortable situations into occasions for learning and broadening students' understanding of themselves and others.

9. Sense of Being a Part of History

As we have proposed throughout the book, service can have a powerful impact on youth's identity development when it fosters a sense of relatedness to society and larger historical processes. Just as the literature on participation in the civil rights movement (Fendrich 1993; McAdam 1988) and the Peace Corps (Stein 1966) has shown, youth become invested in service when they believe that their actions are helping to make history. On the other hand, it is also easy to understand how youth can maintain the disengaged role of voyeur when service is treated as an isolated or decontextualized event.

Three characteristics of the St. Francis program helped to foster a sense of historicism. First, the course curriculum emphasized that students' actions were part of a historical religious perspective. Applying

Catholic principles, specifically the theologies of Karl Rahner and Pierre Teilhard de Chardin, Mr. Siwek told students that they were part of an evolutionary process moving humanity closer to God. He argued that by doing something that was not the contemporary norm, such as becoming people who care about homelessness, students were moving all of humanity forward.

Second, much of the course content consisted in the history of activist movements in the United States. Moral exemplars were presented as historical figures who were ahead of their time and pushed humanity forward. Students learned about Martin Luther King Jr.'s leadership in the civil rights movement, Cesar Chavez's struggle to improve the conditions of farm laborers, and Mitch Snyder's efforts to bring the plight of the homeless to the nation's consciousness. Mr. Siwek placed significant emphasis on Martin Luther King Jr., who he said had a profound impact on his own life. In doing this, he offered a model from the recent history of Blacks in the United States in order to encourage students to become part of a tradition of activism.

A third characteristic of the program that helped students to feel part of a historical process was the long-term relationship between St. Francis and the soup kitchen. For 18 years, students from St. Francis had performed the same service at the same soup kitchen, although it changed location in the late 1980s. In this way, the experience of members of individual junior classes was a tangible part of the school's lore. Articulating this view, student 701 wrote at the end of her final essay in May: "There was no best moment for me today. Every moment I spent there, I spent as my last representation to St. Francis."

10. Responsibility

Recently, educators and policy makers have voiced concern that adolescents tend to focus more on the freedoms of citizenship in a democracy than on the responsibilities (Kennedy 1991; People for the American Way 1989). We challenged some of these arguments in chapter 1 by pointing out that many adolescents are currently active members within their communities, and we believe our data illustrate further that service can foster a sense of social responsibility. Certainly, the concept of responsibility resonated throughout the year in the St. Francis program. Classroom discourse, students' essays, and discussion groups, all explored questions of personal and social responsibility. In the classroom, Mr. Siwek worked to make responsibility the primary theme of his course. The course textbook included the following statement on the course philosophy: "In the final analysis, *either we care about these problems or we do not*. If you do care, then you will want to know more, to be informed, to be able to think critically, and thus be prepared to make your response to this world." To add authoritative power, on the bottom of the same page, he placed an excerpt from Martin Luther King Jr.'s final sermon: "For when people get caught up with that which is right, and they are willing to sacrifice for it, there is no stopping point short of victory" (King 1986, 281).

One way Mr. Siwek kept the theme of responsibility present throughout the year was by emphasizing lines from videos shown during class. In September, while viewing a *60 Minutes* news segment on depleting services for the homeless, Mr. Siwek paused the tape to emphasize a statement made by the commentator. Standing next to the video monitor, Mr. Siwek stated, "This is a line that you must memorize, 'A society is really judged by how it treats its least desirable people.' Not by its highways. No."

In April, Mr. Siwek repeated this practice of pausing the video. Students were watching a documentary called *Common Threads* on the making of the AIDS quilt. After a segment showing an interview with one of the quilt organizers who had AIDS, Mr. Siwek stopped the tape and repeated the organizer's words: "If I live another ten minutes or ten years, that's how I'm going to spend my time. Agitating because change needs to happen." Mr. Siwek then added his own appeal for students to take up the challenge of personal responsibility to enact social justice: "Agitate, agitate, be a thorn in someone's side."

Students did not simply accept Mr. Siwek's interpretation of social problems; rather their essays and discussion groups reveal that they actively struggled with notions of responsibility. Student 304's first essay illustrates the complexity of thoughts and emotions concerning issues of responsibility evoked by service at the soup kitchen. His essay portrays his effort to integrate ideas from the soup kitchen, class, and previous personal experiences.

> I was told, 'Thank you' over and over again. Really, that's about the only time that I felt like I was doing something right, except for a long time ago when I taught a lady's daughter on the bus how to say her ABCs. Everyone on the bus was smiling at me and clapping. And I felt like these people were clapping for me too, but in a different way . . . I grew up around [streets

in an impoverished inner-city area]. My life was 'eat this, eat that, don't waste s---.' But some how and some way we made it out. We went from a filthy apartment littered with vermin to a nice house [in a middle-class neighborhood]. But I just can't seem to figure out where we got the break. But who is going to give them a break? . . . But it was more than an assignment. It was a face to face meeting with reality. Now I see why you can't be a 5, even a 3, 4, 6, 7, 8, 9, or 2. There should be only ones or tens [idea Mr. Siwek discussed in class]. If you are going to accept something, you should accept it whole heartedly. But if you don't like it, then have the guts to come out and say it . . . I'm still in-between. But me being in-between ain't going to help the world any. What I do know is that people shouldn't just sit back and let this happen.

This student's experiences at the soup kitchen provoked him to find a meaningful response to the moral dilemmas of poverty and inequity. The fate of less fortunate others was no longer a distant issue. His essay describes a process through which questions of responsibility took on greater importance as they became increasingly personalized.

Conclusion

The ten ideas outlined above are directed at helping service programs to engage youth and encourage them to be active members in society. All of these ideas seem important from the perspective of adolescent identity development. They incorporate some of the unique characteristics of this developmental period in which abilities for theoretical reflection become more pronounced as youth attempt to define their role within a social framework extending beyond family and friends.

In accordance with this perspective, service programs should provide opportunities for youth to become part of a group combating real social needs. Recognizing the unique opportunities that service provides, the goals of service should be oriented toward helping others and becoming more connected to others. The goals of service programs should be consistent with the founding principles of the organization that implements the program. By offering a ideological framework, organizations enable youth to reflect on the value of these principles, and this process can promote a heightened sense of membership within a group working for a cause or, at least, challenge youth to come up with alternate solutions to social problems.

Opportunities for these types of reflection should take place in both private and public contexts. Public reflection, in particular, can lead to new insights as peers challenge and elaborate upon each other's ideas. Adults such as program organizers and site supervisors also play an important role in encouraging engagement and reflectivity; programs should make use of their enthusiasm and knowledge. Programs also need to recognize social diversity in youth's backgrounds, which can influence the types of experiences that they have. Service organized in this way provides a concrete vehicle for promoting a sense of membership within a historical framework as well as fostering social responsibility.

The St. Francis program has been developed over many years into a program in which the classroom and service are integrated. Efforts have been directed at making the program a defining aspect of the identity of the school and its members. The challenge of implementing a program like St. Francis's is daunting. Enormous commitment, particularly of service organizers, is required. Yet establishing this kind of program can also yield vast rewards. Mr. Siwek clearly took great pride in the alumni's memories of the junior-year social justice course and the soup kitchen (chapter 8). When service programs like the one at St. Francis are implemented, they have enormous potential for positively influencing youth's understanding that they have a role to play in enacting positive change in society.

CHAPTER TEN

Identities in the Making

In this concluding chapter, we discuss our findings by integrating them with the major themes that were introduced at the beginning of the book. Educators and policy analysts want to know whether service is useful and, if it is, how its benefits are mediated. Psychologists and sociologists need to know more about the processes by which effects of service are produced and contribute to identity development. Although we studied only a single group of adolescents, we believe the findings are relevant to adolescents in general. The task of establishing a social-historically coherent identity is not peculiar to the students we studied but common for all youth. The primarily Black, middle-class students we studied face the same hurdles to identity that other contemporary urban youth confront in having limited access to social structures in which their talents for making history can be tested. We recognize, of course, that the St. Francis students face additional challenges because of racism in our society. We consider this matter at the end of the chapter, but for the present, we assume that our findings are applicable to contemporary youth who are in the midst of constructing social-historically meaningful identities.

We began this book by trying to combat caricatures of contemporary youth as hedonistic and disinterested in normative society. Ample empirical evidence indicates that the majority of the present youth cohort is positively oriented to the social norms held by older generations but generally lacks the means to express this orientation. Our social institutions tend not to take account of youth's talents, but shunt them off to school where students are told to mark time while preparing for adulthood. We believe our results support those scholars who have recognized youth's assets and have argued that youth ought to be given direct opportunities to experience themselves in the history-making process. Youth would thereby develop confidence in their agency, accept social responsibility, and advance their political-moral socialization. All of these, we propose, constitute identity as the whole individual is incorporated into mature social membership.

154

Our assessment of this theory was based on students' reflections and understandings of work at the soup kitchen and the phenomenon of homelessness. In interpreting their service, students began to explore their present and prospective relations to society. Experiences at the soup kitchen were integrated with classroom instruction, as students clarified their stance toward the political and moral order in which homelessness was a social fact and a challenge to their inquiring minds. The present chapter discusses what we learned from the St. Francis service program. Using our theoretical framework, we hope to show what might be achieved for any youth who were given similar service experiences during the developmentally opportune era of adolescence.

The Unity of Service and Program

The service activity and instructional program in which it was embedded cannot be separated when assessing effects on the participants. Although the St. Francis program is a single case, it is instructive with regard to Erikson's argument that industry, or action, is essential for identity development, and needs to be coupled with clear ideological guidelines for appraising experience. Youth may accept or reject particular ideological positions, but once they start to ask questions about society's makeup, ideological nourishment is required for orienting their reflective reasoning. The social justice class provided students with a Judeo-Christian rationale for service, made even more specific in terms of a *Catholic ethic* (Tropman 1995). In this view, instrumental action, or work, is considered more in terms of its impact on the community than of its benefit to the individual actor. Moreover, the obligation to act on behalf of less fortunate others is the key to participating in a respected tradition of social justice, which was exemplified through government leaders such as Franklin D. Roosevelt, religious leaders such as Martin Luther King Jr., and idealistic champions of the poor such as Dorothy Day, Cesar Chavez, and Mitch Snyder.

As noted in the previous chapter, program specialists recognize the complementarity of instructional and reflective components in service curricula. Our results show the advantage of directing reflection to ideological alternatives through which youth can connect themselves to history. It is important to discover the power of one's agency, but even more valuable to see one's agency coupled with that of previous generations. This provides access to the transcendent dimension that is necessary for identity to gain respect and have stable meaning. Identity cannot be founded on personal experience alone, which is ephemeral and subject to emotional fluctuations. By partaking in ideological positions that have historical legitimacy, youth can come to share in collective meanings that ground identity in a truly social way.

It is futile to ask whether work at the soup kitchen or the social justice class was the more effective component for our students. One depended on and complemented the other, when either alone would surely have been less effective in promoting development. Service offered experience in instrumental competence, and the social justice class provided ideological clarity. Hence, the practice of agency and responsibility was coupled with a cognitive and affective understanding of justice.

For purposes of our theory, it is crucial that students served the homeless, rather than just reading about or hearing lectures about homelessness. This is because development is paced by action and persons' understanding of their actions in relation to the social context. The key to identity is to know what can be accomplished through individual and collective actions within a group of like-minded actors. To paraphrase Erikson, identity advances when youth can experience themselves doing things well and doing them together and, we add, when the doing serves a transcendent purpose.

Reflective Reasoning

Much of what youth do in their daily ventures has little meaning beyond the immediate moment. Working with homeless persons helped move attention beyond the momentary self. Experiences at the kitchen put students in touch with the problematic side of society and with the consequences of lives gone awry. Students were primed to think about causes and conditions for problems and to imagine solutions for which they and society may have responsibility.

There were several reasons the St. Francis students may have found homelessness a cognitively and affectively provocative topic. One group of reasons pertains to a possible identification with the homeless. For example, some diners were young Black males who had recently completed high school but were unemployed. Thus, seeing them presented students with a personally relevant occasion to question their own future job prospects. Another group of reasons that the soup-kitchen experience was provocative concerns the contradiction that homelessness presented to students' idealism. As we noted, the kitchen was located only minutes from the U.S. capitol, the symbol of the wealthiest and most powerful government in the world. At least some students remarked in their essays that a nation able to build a space program and spend billions of dollars on defense ought to be able to eliminate homelessness.

Insofar as students were empathetic to the people they met at the kitchen and wanted to understand the phenomenon of homelessness, the logical next question was, what should be done now? The social justice class and kitchen supervisors provided students with a long list of persons and institutions that ought to be involved in ending homelessness and remediating its effects. In essays and discussions, students repeated some of the nominees, but more important, students did their own probing in trying to come to a satisfactory understanding. If students were merely repeating what they had heard, there would have been greater consensus about responsible parties and feasible remedial action. Instead, students vigorously debated causes and likely solutions. Indeed, students' questions of responsibility and what should be done remained continuing topics throughout the year and typically led to heated exchanges between advocates of various positions.

Reflective Processes

The psychological literature has gone through two recent phases on the matter of reflectivity. Piaget's writings (see Furth 1969) distinguish reflective reasoning from simple internalization of experience. Reality is not given, but individuals construct it by reflecting on their actions in order to make sense of past experience and anticipate their future actions. Knowledge is not a copy of things or of actions, but a mental construction designed to model how the world is and should be.

More recently, this notion has been moved forward in an interesting elaboration of Vygotsky's writings (e.g., Wertsch 1985). Not only is reflection an individual activity, it is also a social process in which two or more individuals reason together in the sense-making process. Knowledge is founded on personal experience plus reflection that occurs in social interaction with others (Youniss and Damon 1992). One can further suggest that society possesses knowledge and tools for knowledge that can be used for individual cognitive gains (Cole and Wertsch

1996). It follows that individual development is due to the person's effort but supported and directed by social enabling conditions.

Our data show that students manifested reflection in their essays and discussions and that the two had similar effects. Essays were presumably written privately in an effort to understand a day's experiences at the kitchen, and they evoked transcendent reflections as was shown in chapters 4–7. These reflections were abetted by cultural tools such as those the teachers provided. Focus on the political and moral sides of homelessness was prodded by the social justice class. Still, it was the students who used the tools to reorder what had happened at the kitchen and to make sense of their experience. For example, several students recounted the bizarre behavior of transvestites at the kitchen in what appeared to be honest amazement with a new and riveting aspect of life. Students used the essays to describe what they saw and to raise questions about homosexuality and their attitudes toward it.

Reflection was equally evident in the discussion sessions. Individual students frequently made evaluative statements to their peers as they had done in their essays. Had we videotaped the discussions, we might have been able to match individuals' essays with their input during discussions. Nevertheless, group discussions provided valuable insight into the reflective process almost as if it were drawn out elaborately in slow motion through turn taking. Ideas were exchanged publicly and sequentially so that one could see them taking shape and being revised (Youniss and Yates 1996).

Four broad types of exchanges depict the reflective process.

Validation. When one student offered an interpretation of an event at the kitchen, other students often verified it with reference to the same event or to a comparable event from their day at the kitchen. Intersubjective validation helps to deter getting enmeshed in subjective mazes. Validation also occurred in the essay material when students verified in later visits to the kitchen what they had seen in earlier visits. There seems to be more efficiency in discussion, however, because the experiences of several students can be compared and contrasted simultaneously and instantaneously.

Challenge. In contrast to validation, one student's interpretation of an event was often challenged by other students who offered contradictory or alternate interpretations. In some instances, interpretations were defended, which led to extended exchanges that moved toward mutual agreement. Challenges also appeared in the essays, for example, when individuals noted how experiences forced them to alter their prior viewpoints, such as their stereotypes of homeless people. Nevertheless, discussion has advantages over private reflection because initial interpretations are literally pulled apart by oppositional data. Challenges were easy to see in group discussions as various students holding legitimately opposing views expressed them in a mix that forced rethinking of ideas.

A major role for challenges is to show that there are several interpretations of any factual event. Students debated one another, for example, about whether teenage mothers on welfare should work or continue their education, and whether prisoners should be punished for their crimes or educated so as to become employable. As noted in chapter 7, heated disagreements also followed any mention of stereotypes of Black youth, with some students pointing to empirical facts and others citing the distinctions that had to be made among types of teenagers. In summary, challenges afforded the examples of what developmental theory holds to be the primary function of reflectivity. They forced individuals to compare and clarify interpretations instead of maintaining an immediate and singular view that might not have held up to further experience.

Resolution. Challenges sometimes led to exchanges in which students took and held opposing viewpoints, resulting in stalemate. One example pertained to whether one should give money to homeless people, with one side saying no, because they might use it for drugs or alcohol, and the other side saying yes, because they need it for food and other things. Both views were grounded in students' experience with homeless people and thus had legitimacy. On several occasions when such stalemates arose, third parties often entered the debate to offer resolutions that would satisfy both sides but would, in principle, raise the discussion to a more productive level. In the case of whether to give homeless people money, for instance, one student offered a resolution that emphasized the purpose of giving rather than its possible consequences. This student argued that one should give according to the need of the recipient and not pay attention to what the recipient might do. If the intention of giving money is to help, it does not matter what the recipient does.

Leaving differences unresolved. Although resolutions occurred frequently, it was just as common that opposing viewpoints were not resolved. This, of course, happens in private reflection also. There are cases when contradictory experiences cannot be reconciled, and when one set of facts supports one interpretation while another set supports a different perspective. This occurred in group discussions not so much with facts as with ways to interpret events. For instance, some students viewed themselves as "realists" while viewing others as "naive." Topics such as drug peddling or teenage violence were apt to bring out this view of differences among classmates. At a point when the irreconcilability was tacitly acknowledged, a new topic was introduced, with the previous differences remaining as they were. This kind of reflection occurred in essays when students presented alternate interpretations of events. However, it is difficult to say whether different views were being carefully weighed, as in discussions, or if students were merely confused about possible interpretations.

Intersubjectivity and Collective Identity

Although reflections in essays and discussions are parallel in function, the latter have two distinctive features that merit further consideration. First, whereas private reflection serves the purpose of coordinating thoughts within an individual, reflection through discussion helps to coordinate thoughts among individuals. In exchanging ideas, arguing, defending points of view, and the like, students implicitly work toward mutual understanding. Students often were not simply exchanging ideas in turn, but were trying to persuade one another toward particular points of view. This was especially true when racial matters were brought up and stereotypes of Black youth were mentioned. In those instances, students challenged one another and seemed to be arguing about right and wrong ways to view Black youth. Their aim was to persuade those with the "wrong" view to change perspectives toward a proper one for this group to share. The result, whether intended or not, was to promote the possibility of intersubjective agreement, or mutual understanding of one another's views.

The second distinctive feature followed from mutual understanding. When students tried to achieve consensus, or at least shared understanding, they were implicitly promoting collective beliefs. This was evident in the frequent use of moral framing of issues (Gamson 1992). Quite often, topics were introduced in an oppositional fashion, with one view being favored over another that was cast as morally incorrect. According to Gamson (1992), the tactic of framing debate in terms of moral indignation helps to engage the participants and fosters collective identity in the sense that one view is presented as appropriate for the group. For example, when students discussed the possibility that the church building that housed the kitchen might be torn down for urban renewal, they framed the issue in terms of heartless developers versus church leaders who were working for social justice. The aim of this framing was to emphasize the moral correctness on the church's part and to argue that right-thinking people should go along with it. Students who used this tactic were effectively saying that members of the social justice class were obliged to uphold certain outlooks, because they shared a common moral perspective. Hence, in arguing aloud for one or another position, students were working toward shared understanding and promoting collective identity.

Doing as a Form of Socialization

The topic of reflective reasoning leads directly to the matter of socialization and how we interpret the impact of service and classroom instruction. We have argued that development occurs as students construct a relationship with society. This relationship is not a copy of what students were taught in class, heard from peers, or observed at the kitchen. While the classroom and the kitchen provided objective material for thought, students submitted it to reflection in which they compared and coordinated interpretations in order to make sense of their experiences. Through these constructions the conjunction of service and the social justice class advanced socialization toward mature political-moral identity.

According to a microsociological approach (chapter 2), children and youth acquire knowledge through the use of personal action and social interaction (Tesson and Youniss 1995). Armed with these tools, students adopt and hone action routines that become the core material that defines their collective society (e.g., Corsaro and Eder 1990). Participating in these routines, students become members of the group, with knowledge of how to operate effectively within it. Thus, this theory readily explains how children and youth form collectives in which meaning is shared and a healthy social life is lived. This approach grants children control over their own understandings of society. It is achieved by recognizing that macrosociological structures exist, but have an impact only insofar as people act them out in every-day practice. While people's practices are affected by structures, these structures depend wholly on people's practices, without which the structures would be moot.

We find this approach useful because it acknowledges the existence of political and moral structures, but puts the burden for understanding and constituting them on the actions of youth. Accordingly, service at the kitchen gave students occasion to partake of political and moral practices that are normative for adults and prepare them for entering adult society. However, adult society cannot impose itself on children and youth but must be reconstituted by them as they try to make sense of their actions in the world.

For example, we argued that students were developing senses of agency and social responsibility that are essential for democratic citizenship (chapter 5). At the level of practices, democracy involves learning to express one's views, listening to others' views, tolerating differences, acquiring the skills of arguing reasonably, seeking compromises, and acceding to legitimate majority views. Democracy has to be more than abstraction that is stated in formal terms if youth are to incorporate it into their understandings of society. It depends wholly on their acquiring democratic practices. Were these practices not to take place, democracy as a formal structure would dwindle away. An instructive example is found in Eastern Europe; when people stopped acting in socialist form, the governing structures had to give way. This occurred in 1989, when East German citizens carried candles to Nicolai Church to pronounce the end of the socialist state, and Czech citizens rattled their keys in Wenceslas Square to mark the end of fascism. When people stop acting in accord with formal political structures, political regimes are no longer viable.

The studies we cited in chapter 2 on long-term effects of participation in high school–based activities present a case that supports this theory. High school students who were involved in school government were found to partake of political activity and to be less alienated from the political sphere as adults than were adults who had not participated during their high school years (e.g., Hanks and Eckland 1978; Otto 1976). A recent study by Verba, Schlozman, and Brady (1995) confirms this finding with retrospective accounts from a sample of 2,517 adults. The strongest predictor of adults' current political activism was their participation in high school government and nonathletic school groups and clubs. In the authors' terms, "American high schools [provide] hands-on training for future participation . . . They give opportunities to practice democratic governance" (425).

By viewing the St. Francis students prospectively, we can see their present political and moral practices as training for adult life. By political practices, we mean no more than what Collins (1979), Gamson (1992), and Verba, Schlozman, and Brady (1995) have defined as properly political. These practices include students' recognition that there are political aspects to homelessness, for instance, housing policies, zoning decisions, urban redevelopment, job-training programs, and the like. They also include being able to present and discuss political viewpoints intelligently so that ideas are articulated clearly and exchanged convincingly with one's equals.

In chapter 5, we emphasized the development of agency and social responsibility as two major aspects of political socialization. Again, a look at the former socialist states in Eastern Europe helps make the point that these components need to be socialized and do not arise automatically in adulthood. The official change in government did not and could not instantly produce democracy, because the citizens still had to learn how to act democratically, having lived for 50 years under a system that did not promote political participation (Noack, Hofer, and Youniss 1995).

Democratic routines such as demonstrating or voting have to be made part of the definition of the democratic self for the government to acquire the same definition. Thus, St. Francis students' practice of elemental political routines gives insight into basic steps toward adult political identity. Verba, Schlozman, and Brady's (1995, 528) depiction of mature political behavior provides a clear point of reference for what we observed in the St. Francis students: "In a fuller participatory democracy, political activity becomes a mechanism whereby citizens engage in enlightened discourse, come to understand the views of others, and become sensitized to the needs of the community and nation. Thus educated, they transcend their narrow interests to seek the public good."

Toren (1993), an anthropologist, has described this approach to socialization with a different label, *microhistory*, to emphasize that children and youth literally take their place in a society's history by carrying on from where adults have left it. She proposes that children and youth need to construct the world, starting from the political-economic structures they are given, to advance history in the next generation. The world they constitute "is at once the same as, *and different from,* the world their elders know" (463). She uses the term "embodied engagement" to emphasize that socialization consists in the practice of those routines that define structures in adult society. Yet the structures are never exactly duplicated because the process of generational renewal is novel for each generation. Consequently, children and youth are the producers of history, even though they build on the society the previous generation has given them.

Socialization of the sort we saw at St. Francis is not a matter of reciting facts from textbooks in civics or religion. It consists in *doing* politics and *doing* morality. Students practiced routines that, at once, came from existing political and moral traditions but were reconstituted by students in light of their experience. These students were then partaking of their generational role and making use of their agency to create and renew society. And, having taken a hand in remaking society, these students took the additional step of accepting responsibility for society and wanting to make it more just.

The Structure of Identity

Recent work in the area of moral development has shifted from the study of judgment to investigation of the lives of people who are involved in principled social activism and community service (Flanagan 1991). The rationale for this position has been argued ably by Blasi (1984, 1995), who uses the concept of identity to make his case. For Blasi, morality does not consist in thought or in action alone, but is a characteristic of persons. Morality belongs to individuals insofar as they have identities that link them to society. According to Blasi (1984, 130), "Morality is more characteristic of the agent than of either action or thinking; the ultimate source of goodness lies in good will, and good will is at the core of what a person is."

Blasi (1995) proposes that morality and self develop somewhat separately during childhood but become more integrated during adolescence when identity comes to the fore. One imagines this is true also for political reasoning, from which young children are considerably distanced (Furth 1980). But as adolescents attend to their identities, they must confront the political and moral dimensions of the society they are entering. The work of identity, as we have been arguing, is to form a self that integrates these dimensions when this requires locating the self within respected ideological traditions. This task involves going beyond one's personal experiences to find transcendent meaning that provides ideal perspectives that can be taken toward the self's and society's future.

Two recent studies illustrate this theoretical perspective in interesting ways. Hart and Fegley (1995) describe 15 adolescents who were notable for their extraordinary commitment to altruistic service in their community of Camden, New Jersey. These adolescents were nominated by church leaders and heads of local service organizations and were interviewed about their rationale for service. One important finding is that these adolescents described themselves with direct mention of their moral commitment to service. Morality had priority for their self-concept, in contrast to a matched comparison group of adolescents who did no service. Another finding of interest is that these youth did not view their altruism as noteworthy or remarkable. They took for granted that voluntary service was part of who they were as persons. Their service did not merit special mention because it had become taken for granted in their self-definition (see also Hart and Yates 1997).

Colby and Damon (1992, 1995) reported a comparable study of 23 American adults who had been nominated by a panel of experts as "moral exemplars" for having led highly moral lives in the service of other people. As with Hart and Fegley's adolescents, these adults did not view their service as extraordinary. According to Colby and Damon (1995, 363), "The most noteworthy thing about these behaviors is their very unnoteworthiness. They are performed habitually, as a matter of course." Additionally, Colby and Damon concluded that a general finding across the 23 exemplars was an apparent "*[u]nity of self and moral goals,* which refers to the central place of the exemplars' moral goals in their conceptions of their own identity" (362).

We did not study the self-concept as such in our students but found ample evidence that concurs with these results. Several students saw their service in moral and political terms and saw themselves developing into social activists. It is relevant to their identity that several students pictured themselves in the future as adults who would work to solve society's problems from then-achieved more powerful social roles. Further, we saw that several alumni continued to think of themselves as political and moral actors serving society by redressing its social ills. For example, one young alumna said she wanted to use her skills to start a program for the homeless that would gain them employment and self-sufficiency. For her, service would become a career in which she provided homeless persons with job skills and counseling that would enable them to live normal lives.

We do not say that a full integration was evident in our students. We propose only that their practices and reasoning about homelessness represented steps toward integrated moral identities. At a minimum, we think our data represent early steps toward this goal. The St. Francis program gave students numerous opportunities for appraising possible political and moral practices and ideals for their emerging self-definitions. We believe the findings support a theory in which politics and morality are studied as parts of identity instead of as separate domains or behaviors. Perhaps the clearest examples were found in chapter 6, when students argued for fair treatment of the homeless, not only citing principles of justice, but coupling them with compassion. Wanting to help others because they share in a common humanity epitomizes an identity in which moral ideals are an inseparable part of the self, which is, in turn, defined in its relationship to society.

Race and Humanity

We now turn to ethnicity, or race, as another fundamental part of identity. It was shown in chapter 7 that students spent considerable energy discussing race in an ongoing debate about what it means to be Black. We assume that answering this question is essential to establishing identity for these youth. They live in a society in which color marks them as different and saddles them with preassigned biases and perceptions they must learn to reject, defend against, and otherwise master. While being Black in contemporary America automatically assigns one to a social group, it does not automatically grant a sense of personal meaning or group belonging. To attain a meaningful Black identity, students must work to make sense of their experiences in light of the personal and collective past and future they are constructing.

We emphasize two themes in the following discussion. One is that the task of establishing Black identity and figuring out what it means to be Black is complex and effortful. This is because students themselves have different ideas on the meaning of Blackness, if only because of their diverse backgrounds. Differences are also due to a range of possible answers to the question of what it means to be Black. The other theme is that, while defining Blackness is a primary task, so too is dealing with the task of becoming members of society, which involves transcending color. According to the ethic of the social justice course, the principles of justice and expression of compassion apply to all who share a common humanity.

Differences and Commonalities

Regarding different viewpoints among the students, we note that they came from different family backgrounds, were mixed in terms of social class, belonged to different religious denominations, and so forth. It is understandable, then, that they expressed varied judgments and took oppositional sides in discussions of several issues, for example, the need for welfare reform, proper treatment of prisoners, and causes of homelessness. Students differed also in their appraisals of Black public figures, including politicians, wealthy athletes, and entertainment stars. These differences were often expressed in moral terms, for example, when students disagreed about whether athletes deserve million-dollar salaries. Do salaries belong solely to the athletes or should they be used to help the community? Arguments centered on the brevity of athletic careers, the example set by athletes who contribute back to communities, and the inappropriateness of judging others.

Background differences among students were coupled with two sources of unity that may have helped them to establish a sense of collective Black identity. One was what Marable (1995) refers to as the stable coordinates of White-Black opposition in our society. If students had nothing else in common, they shared minority status in a society with a White majority. Students showed consciousness of this by making numerous comparisons to their White counterparts in other high schools. For example, they compared themselves positively to students from elite White schools who were occasional volunteers at the soup kitchen. The St. Francis students commented on how little work these other students did and that those students were shocked to discover that any of the homeless diners were White. Another example pertained to the rising cost of tuition at St. Francis and the possibility that wealthy White students might replace the Black student body.

The second source of unification was students' awareness that they were participants in a positive tradition of Black upward mobility. St. Francis high school itself was a sign of this success, with over 97% of its current graduates having gone on to college. As we noted earlier, students made repeated references to the accomplishments of St. Francis in athletics, academics, and community service. Students described themselves as "St. Francis students" with obvious pride. This was evident when they referred to encounters with homeless persons who offered a "thank you" and knowingly added, "you must be from St. Francis."

Part of the mobility ethos extended to students' recognition of partaking in the next era of the civil rights struggle that their grandparents and parents had forged in the 1950s and 1960s. This struggle was an important section of the social justice course and gave students historical grounding that enabled them to achieve transcendent meaning. Seeing one's generation as partaking in the same ideological cause as the older generation is an obvious resource that strengthens identity formation. To paraphrase one student on this point, we know what our parents' generation went through. We now have a different society to deal with in our own struggle to keep working for social justice.

Manning Marable (1995, 6) has provided a moving and apt biographical depiction of these issues, which illuminates the complex task identity presents for Black youth.

> To be black in what seems to be a bipolar racial universe gives one instantly a set of coordinates within space and time, a sense of geographical location along an endless boundary of color. Blackness as a function of the racial superstructure also gives meaning to collective memory. It allows us to place ourselves within a context of racial resistance, within the many struggles for human dignity, for our families and for material resources. This consciousness of racial pride and community awareness gave hope and strength to my grandfather and father; it was also the prime motivation for the Edward Wilmot Blydens, Marcus Garveys, and Fannie Lou Hamers throughout black history. In this way, the prism of race structures the community of the imagination, setting parameters for real activity and collective possibility.

It is important to recognize that students discussed issues pertaining to Black identity regularly and intensely. This promoted its individual and collective sides. Discussion of Black issues assured that identity would be as much collective as individual, in process as well as outcome. While identity requires personal resolution of the forgoing questions, it equally involves defining oneself in terms of the larger group, which ranges from Black teenagers in Washington, DC, to reviewing the history of prior generations and race relations in America (Cross 1995a, 1995b; Fordham 1996; Spencer and Dornbusch 1990). To be Black is thus not simply to adopt an available model or to band together with other people of color. To form a Black identity is a conscious act of understanding and becoming part of a people with a shared history, a sense of achievement under difficult odds, and an outlook to the future that combines cautious realism with legitimate hope (Marable 1995). It is this history with its message of agency and responsibility that allows students to form a Black identity, yet to be individual, and to look to the future with optimism.

Transcending Polarized Identities

The extension of collective identity to all of society was encouraged by the St. Francis program, in which the concept of social justice applied to all humanity and was not limited by race, familiarity, ethnicity, or religion. Students were encouraged to consider adopting this tradition, which has respected religious and cultural roots. This urging produced several moments of tension during the year, for example, when the Nation of Islam and Louis Farrakhan were mentioned. For instance, in one discussion session, some students decried the separatism that Farrakhan promoted while other students recounted the good works the Nation of Islam had done in Washington's poorer neighborhoods. A special occurrence helped to focus this issue when a former Nation of Islam minister, Khalid Muhammad, delivered a racially inflammatory speech in Washington (see chapter 7). In response, Mr. Siwek contrasted Muhammad's speech with those of Martin Luther King Jr., who called for one brotherhood with Catholics and Jews. He also assigned a visit to the Holocaust Museum in order to show that hatred and injustice were not exclusively aimed at Blacks.

While the universality of humanity was essential to the integrity of the theology of the social justice curriculum (Tropman 1995), we cannot specify how far students had moved toward the *we* that included all of humanity. We saw glimpses that it might have taken root when students expressed compassion for the homeless and poor people, in general. While students noted that Blacks were disproportionately represented at the kitchen, they acknowledged that homelessness affected all races. At the same time, homelessness brought focus to issues affecting Black youth and adults, as we noted several times. Hence, it is one thing to ask students to identify with all humanity, but quite another to ask adolescents who are contending with racism, worrying about employment opportunities, and facing daily neighborhood violence, to work for justice for all people.

It is recognized at the same time that achievement of *we* requires work on the part of all others, especially the White majority. Our approach to socialization, then, would encourage service in which Whites and Blacks would confront unequal power relations in society and work to remediate social problems. Attainment of a sense of a more universal *we* requires an approximation through more universal collective action aimed at transforming society.

Citizens Who Can Make History

Marable (1995) and West (1993) have warned of, and Wilson (1987) has documented the consequences of, nihilism that has come from decades of segregation of minorities and impoverished people in our urban centers. Fine (1991) has shown how schools can unwittingly foster, rather than counteract, hopelessness in minority youth. Noting national statistics on high school graduation, she offers an insider's view from a 21-year-old school dropout named Tony: "We need to tell little kids to reach for the impossible. But then they get to school and learn only about what they can't do. What's not possible" (10).

St. Francis in general and the social justice teachers in particular encouraged students to accept the responsibility to work toward a just world by using their talents for political reform with moral compassion. The students' age, race, apparent lack of power, and inexperience were not to be used to shirk this obligation. In the Catholic ethic being fostered, responsibility for advancing social justice was shared by everyone for the common good, which prevails over individual benefits (Bryk, Lee, and Holland 1993).

We recognize the need to be cautious here because the topic of Catholic school education for non-Catholic minority students has generated considerable controversy among social scientists. The work of James Coleman and his colleagues (e.g., Coleman and Hoffer 1987) has been viewed by some critics as an unfair attack on public schools that undermines the nation's confidence in them. Coleman et alia reported that Black students in parochial schools, on average, score higher on achievement tests than their Black peers in public schools. They also reported that Black students in parochial schools are less likely to drop out of school and to manifest antisocial behaviors than their public school peers.

Critics have pointed out problems with this comparison by noting, for example, that parents who send their adolescents to parochial high schools might have exceptional academic expectations and guide their adolescents accordingly. Such parents also are probably committed to values that are concordant with those of the schools; hence, they create a virtual community that reinforces desired behaviors consistently. Further, parochial schools, as opposed to public schools, can control enrollment by imposing entrance requirements and exerting discipline. Witness the immediate dismissal of the male found with a handgun in the St. Francis parking lot and of three more juniors for other offenses during the year.

Bryk, Lee, and Holland (1993) have offered a new perspective on this controversy by describing what, in fact, goes on inside these schools as academic material and values are formally taught and actually practiced by administrators, teachers, and students. The present study can be considered an elaboration of this account insofar as we have described the actual workings of the educational process in one class. This approach has an advantage over former studies because it gives insight into process rather than just reporting differences in outcomes between kinds of schools. We are not arguing against public schools, but trying to document a process that, in theory, could be implemented by any kind of school with all types of youth. This is the same advantage offered by Fine's study (1991), which identified processes that, in her case, thwarted students' education, led to their dropping out, and impeded the development of their capacity to secure employment and imagine future lives with optimism.

The St. Francis program exemplified our developmental thesis that encouragement of accepting the task of remaking society can animate the identity process. Students were given a definite ideological structure and a relevant historical framework within which they could find transcendent meaning. Students were not told that politics and government consisted in formal facts or that morality consisted in memorizable religious dicta. Both domains were approached from the perspective that they must be constituted by the students, who have the requisite agency and need to take responsibility for their own and society's future.

Adolescents constitute these domains whether or not parents and schools help them. Adolescents do this because they need to locate their emerging identities within history and society. As Toren (1993) has noted, children and youth have as much at stake in making sense of their world as adults do. But if adolescents are not given help, a danger is that they will find the task confusing and may shy away from sorting through the pluralistic views that make up our society. Another danger is that students will be cowed by the enormity of society's problems and retreat to little niches where their own self-interests can be tended. The St. Francis service program took an assertive approach by presenting the kind of material that Erikson claims adolescents need for resolving their identities: clear ideology based in youth's capacity to act.

Boyte (1991, 765), a critic of "feel-good" community-service programs, argues that "[t]o reengage students in public affairs requires redefining *politics* to include, in addition to electoral activity, ongoing citizen involvement in solving social problems. It requires a conceptual framework that distinguishes between public life and private life. And it calls for a pedagogical strategy that puts the design and ownership of problem-solving projects into the hands of young people." We believe we have shown the developmental wisdom that underlies this plea. Once it is understood that adolescents constitute politics and morality, and once it is understood that the constituting process is integral to identity development, the matters of agency and responsibility follow logically. In this theory, youth do not learn in the abstract about history or take comfort in slogans regarding living in a democratic nation. They remake history as they assess tradition and imagine how they can contribute to making a better society in which they would want to live.

Coles and Brenner (1965) provide an example that fits our approach when they quote a Black student who had participated in Freedom Summer 1964, whose alumni were studied by McAdam (1988). In describing his experience in Mississippi, the student said: "When I go near a voting registrar in Mississippi I feel I'm dueling with the whole history of my race and the white race. It gets you just like that, in your bones. You're not just a person who is scared. You're doing something for the books; for history, too" (910).

Not every generation has the opportunity to grow up during a time of dramatic social change that calls forth idealism and creative energy that reaches people's bones. During 1930–70, youth had obvious occasions to become involved in improvement of work conditions, the national war effort, procurement of civil rights, campus reform, and the like. Youth were mobilized to work together as a generation and to join forces with adults for common purpose. Personal and collective identities were nearly intertwined as exciting roles and effective means were almost handed to youth.

Today, numerous problems remain worthy of youth's efforts and energy. Grassroots social activism is as alive and appropriate today as it was in the past (McAdam, McCarthy, and Zald 1996; O'Neill 1994). Youth today are as talented as they were during the civil rights era. Thus, it is appropriate that the St. Francis program resolutely encouraged students to think of themselves as being *at the right place in the right time* to find their cause and to build their identity. Students were exposed to homelessness as a problem in which several of society's major institutions are implicated. This cause merited their interest and engaged their idealism. Students were told that recognition of injustice and use of their power to redress social problems were part of a noble tradition rooted deeply in Western culture. The St. Francis program proposed to students that, when this tradition was rerooted in them, they would always be in the right place and it would always be the right time to work for social justice with compassion for all.

REFERENCES

Alliance for Service-Learning in Education Reform. 1993. Standards of quality for school-based and community-based service learning. *Equity and Excellence in Education* 26:71–73.

Bachman, G. G., L. D. Johnston, and P. M. O'Malley. 1993. *Monitoring the future: A continuing study of the life styles and values of youth.* Ann Arbor, MI: Survey Research Center.

Barber, B. R., and R. Battistoni. 1993. A season of service: Introducing service learning into the liberal arts curriculum. *PS: Political Science and Politics* 26:235–40.

Baxley, C., and K. Lewis. 1996. Cracks in our values: Community at center of breakdown. *Post and Courier,* January 21, A1.

Berndt, T. J. 1982. The features of friendship in early adolescents. *Child Development* 53:1447–60.

Blasi, A. 1984. Moral identity: Its role in moral functioning. In W. M. Kurtines and J. L. Gewirtz, eds., *Morality, moral behavior, and moral development,* 128–40: New York: Wiley.

———. 1995. Moral understanding and moral personality: The process of moral integration. In W. M. Kurtines and J. L. Gewirtz, eds., *Moral development: An introduction,* 229–53. Needham Heights, MA: Allyn and Bacon.

Boyte, H. C. 1991. Community service and service education. *Phi Delta Kappan* 72:765–67.

Braungart, R. G. 1980. Youth movements. In J. Adelson, ed., *Handbook of adolescence,* 560–97. New York: Wiley.

Brown, B. B. 1990. Peer groups and peer cultures. In S. S. Feldman and G. R. Elliot, eds., *At the threshold: The developing adolescent,* 171–96. Cambridge, MA: Harvard University Press.

Bryk, A. S., V. E. Lee, and P. B. Holland. 1993. *Catholic schools and the common good.* Cambridge, MA: Harvard University Press.

Clary, A. G., and J. Miller. 1986. Socialization and situational influences on sustained altruism. *Child Development* 57:1358–69.

Cognetta, P. V., and N. A. Sprinthall. 1978. Students as teachers: Role taking as a means of promoting psychological and ethical development during adolescence. In N. A. Sprinthall and R. L. Mosher, eds., *Value development as the aim of education,* 53–68. Schenectady: Character Research Press.

Colby, A., and W. Damon. 1992. *Some do care: Contemporary lives of moral commitment.* New York: Free Press.

———. 1995. *The development of extraordinary commitment.* In M. Killen and D. Hart, eds., *Morality in everyday life: Developmental perspectives,* 342–70. New York: Cambridge University Press.

Cole, M., and J. V. Wertsch. 1996. Beyond the individual-social antimony in discussions of Piaget and Vygotsky. *Human Development* 39.

Coleman, J. S. 1961. *The adolescent society.* New York: Free Press.

———. 1987. Families and schools. *Educational Researcher* 16:32–38.

Coleman, J. S., and T. Hoffer. 1987. *Public and private high schools: The impact of communities.* New York: Basic Books.

Coles, R., and J. Brenner. 1965. American youth in a social struggle: The Mississippi Summer project. *American Journal of Orthopsychiatry* 35:909–26.

Collins, R. 1979. *The credential society.* New York: Academic Press.

Commission on National and Community Service. 1993. *What you can do for your country.* Washington, DC: author.

Conrad, D., and D. Hedin. 1982. The impact of experiential education on adolescent development. In D. Conrad and D. Hedin, eds., *Child and Youth Services,* special issue *Youth participation and experiential education,* 4:57–76.

———. 1991. School-based community service: What we know from research and theory. *Phi Delta Kappan* 69:743–49.

Corporation for National and Community Service. 1994. *Principles for high quality national service programs.* Washington, DC: author.

Corsaro, W. 1985. *Friendship and peer culture in the early years.* Norwood, NJ: Ablex.

Corsaro, W., and D. Eder. 1990. Children's peer cultures. *Annual Review of Sociology* 16:197–220.

Cross, W. E. Jr. 1995a. In search of blackness and Afrocentricity: The psychology of Black identity change. In H. W. Harris, H. C. Blue, and E. E. H. Griffith, eds., *Racial and ethnic identity: Psychological development and creative expression,* 53–72. New York: Routledge.

———. 1995b. Oppositional identity and African American youth: Issues and prospects. In W. D. Hawley and A. W. Jackson, eds., *Toward a common destiny,* 185–203. San Francisco: Jossey-Bass.

Davidson, P., and J. Youniss. 1991. Which comes first, morality or identity? In W. M. Kurtines and J. L. Gewirtz, eds., *Handbook of moral development and behavior,* 1:105–21. Hillsdale, NJ: Erlbaum.

Dougherty, D. M. 1993. Adolescent health: Reflections on a report to the U.S. Congress. *American Psychologist* 48:193–201.

Douvan, E., and J. Adelson. 1966. *The adolescent experience.* New York: Wiley.

Eckert, P. 1989. *Jocks and burnouts: Social categories and identity in the high school.* New York: Teachers College Press.

Erikson, E. H. 1958. *Young man Luther: A study in psychoanalysis and history.* New York: Norton.

———. 1968. *Identity: Youth and crisis.* New York: Norton.

———. 1969. *Gandhi's truth on the origins of militant nonviolence.* New York: Norton.

Fasick, F. A. 1984. Parents, peers, youth culture, and autonomy in adolescence. *Adolescence* 19:143–57.

Fendrich, J. 1993. *Ideal Citizens.* Albany: State University of New York Press.

Fine, G. A., J. T. Mortimer, and D. F. Roberts. 1990. Leisure, work, and the mass media. In S. S. Feldman and G. R. Elliot, eds., *At the threshold: The developing adolescent*, 225–52. Cambridge, MA: Harvard University Press.

Fine, M. 1991. *Framing dropouts: Notes on the politics of an urban public high school.* Albany: State University of New York Press.

Flacks, R. 1988. *Making history: The American left and the American mind.* New York: Columbia University Press.

Flanagan, C., and L. S. Gallay. 1995. Reframing the meaning of "political" in research with adolescents. In M. Hepburn, ed., *Perspectives in political science: New directions in political socialization research*, 34–41. New York: Oxford University Press.

Flanagan, O. 1991. *The varieties of moral personality.* Cambridge, MA: Harvard University Press.

Fordham, S. 1996. *Blacked out: Dilemmas of race, identity, and success at Capital High.* Chicago: University of Chicago Press.

The forgotten half: Pathways to success for America's youth and young families. 1988. Washington, DC: William T. Grant Foundation Commission on Work, Family, and Citizenship.

Furth, H. G. 1969. *Piaget and knowledge.* Englewood Cliffs, NJ: Prentice Hall.

———. 1980. *The world of grown-ups.* New York: Elsevier.

Gamson, W. 1992. *Talking politics.* Cambridge, MA: Harvard University Press.

Garcia, J. 1982. Ethnicity and Chicanos: Measurement of ethnic identification, identity, and consciousness. *Hispanic Journal of Behavioral Sciences* 4:295–314.

Gergen, K. J., and M. M. Gergen. 1983. Narratives of the self. In T. R. Sarbin and K. E. Scheibe, eds., *Studies in social identity*, 251–73. New York: Praeger.

Giddens, A. 1993. *New rules of sociological method.* Stanford, CA: Stanford University Press.

Gilbert, J. 1986. *A cycle of outrage: America's reaction to juvenile delinquency in the 1950s.* New York: Oxford University Press.

Gillis, J. 1981. *Youth and history: Tradition and change in European age relations.* New York: Academic Press.

Giroux, H. A. 1996. Hollywood, race, and the demonization of youth: The "kids" are not "alright." *Educational Researcher* 25:31–35.

Gouldner, A. W. 1960. The norm of reciprocity: A preliminary. *American Sociological Review* 25:161–78.

Grotevant, H. D. 1993. The integrative nature of identity: Bringing the soloist into the choir. In J. Kroger, ed., *Discussions on ego identity*, 121–46. Hillsdale, NJ: Erlbaum.

Hamilton, S. 1990. *Apprenticeship for adulthood: Preparing youth for the future.* New York: Free Press.

Hamilton, S., and M. Fenzel. 1988. The impact of volunteer experience on adolescent social development. *Journal of Adolescent Research* 3:65–80.

Hanks, R., and B. K. Eckland. 1978. Adult voluntary associations. *Sociological Quarterly* 19:481–90.

Hart, D., and S. Fegley. 1995. Prosocial behavior and caring in adolescence: Relations to self-understanding and social judgment. *Child Development* 66:1347–59.

Hart, D., and M. Yates. 1997. The interrelation of self and identity in adolescence: A developmental account. In R. Vasta, ed., *Annals of Child Development,* vol. 12, 207–242. London: Jessica Kingsley Publishers.

Hart, D., M. Yates, S. Fegley, and G. Wilson. 1995. Moral commitment in inner-city adolescents. In M. Killen and D. Hart, eds., *Morality in everyday life: Developmental perspectives,* 317–41. New York: Cambridge University Press.

Hartshorne, H., M. A. May, and J. B. Maller. 1929. *Studies in service and self-control.* Vol. 2 of *Studies in the nature of character.* New York: Macmillan.

Haste, H., and J. Torney-Purta, eds. 1992. *The development of political understanding: A new perspective.* New Directions for Child Development, no. 56. San Francisco: Jossey-Bass.

Hodgkinson, V. A., and M. S. Weitzman. 1990. *Volunteering and giving among American teenagers 14 to 17 years of age.* Washington, DC: Independent Sector.

Hogan, R., and N. Emler. 1995. Personality and moral development. In W. M. Kurtines and J. L. Gewirtz, eds., *Moral development: An introduction,* 209–27. Needham Heights, MA: Allyn and Bacon.

Holmes, S. 1996. Income disparity between the poorest and richest rises. *New York Times,* June 20, A1, A18.

Howard, J. A. 1996. Troubled America: A land without wisdom. *Executive Speeches* 10:4–8.

Inhelder, B., and J. Piaget. 1958. *The growth of logical thinking from childhood to adolescence.* New York: Basic Books.

Jahoda, G. 1992. *Crossroads between culture and mind: Continuities and change in theories of human nature.* Cambridge, MA: Harvard University Press.

James, W. [1909] 1971. *The moral equivalent of war and other essays.* New York: Harper and Row.

Kahne, J., and J. Westheimer. 1996. In the service of what? The politics of service learning. *Phi Delta Kappan* 74:593–99.

Kandel, D. B., and G. S. Lesser. 1972. *Youth in two worlds: U.S. and Denmark.* San Francisco: Jossey-Bass.

Keniston, K. 1968. *Young radicals: Notes on committed youth.* New York: Harcourt, Brace, and World.

Kennedy, E. 1991. National service education for citizenship. *Phi Delta Kappan* 72:771–73.

Kett, J. 1977. *Rites of passage.* New York: Basic Books.

Killen, M., and D. Hart, eds. 1995. *Morality in everyday life: Developmental perspectives.* New York: Cambridge University Press.

King, M. L. Jr. 1986. *A testament of hope: The essential writings of Martin Luther King, Jr.* Ed. J. M. Washington. San Francisco: Harper and Row.

Kohlberg, L. 1969. Stage and sequence: The cognitive developmental approach to socialization. In D. A. Goslin, ed., *Handbook of socialization theory and research,* 347–480. Chicago: Rand McNally.

Kropp, A. J. 1994. Kids need responsibility. *USA Today,* April 20, 12A.

Kurtines, W. M., and J. L. Gewirtz, eds. 1995. *Moral development: An introduction.* Needham Heights, MA: Allyn and Bacon.

Ladewig, H., and J. K. Thomas. 1987. *Assessing the impact of 4-H on former members.* College Station: Texas A&M University. Research report.

Larson, R. 1994. Youth organizations, hobbies, and sports as developmental contexts. In R. Silbereisen and E. Todt, eds., *Adolescence in context: The interplay of family, school, peers, and work in adjustment*, 46–65. New York: Springer-Verlag.

Leahy, R. L. 1983. Development of the conception of economic inequality: 2, Explorations, justifications, and concepts of social mobility and change. *Developmental Psychology* 19:111–25.

Lewis, A. 1992. Urban youth in community service: Becoming part of a solution. *Eric/CUE Digest*, no. 81.

Lewko, J. H., ed. 1987. *How children and adolescents view the world of work*. San Francisco: Jossey-Bass.

Logan, R. D. 1985. Youth volunteerism and instrumentality: A commentary, rationale, and proposal. *Journal of Voluntary Action Research* 14:45–50.

Luckmann, T. 1991. The new and old in religion. In P. Bourdieu and J. S. Coleman, eds., *Social theory for a changing society*, 167–88. Boulder, CO: Westview Press.

McAdam, D. 1988. *Freedom summer*. New York: Oxford University Press.

McAdam, D., J. D. McCarthy, and M. N. Zald. 1996. *Comparative perspectives on social movements: Political opportunities, mobilizing structures, and cultural framings*. New York: Cambridge University Press.

MacLeod, J. 1995. *Ain't no makin' it*. Boulder, CO: Westview Press.

Males, M. 1994. Bashing youth: Media myths about teenagers. *Extra*, March–April, 8–11.

Marable, M. 1995. *Beyond Black and White: Transforming African-American politics*. New York: Verso.

Massey, D. S., and N. A. Denton. 1993. *American apartheid: Segregation and the making of the underclass*. Cambridge, MA: Harvard University Press.

Miller, F. 1992. The personal and the political in reasoning and action. In H. Haste and J. Torney-Purta, eds., *The development of political understanding: A new perspective*, 53–63. San Francisco: Jossey-Bass.

National and Community Service Coalition. 1995. *Youth volunteerism: Here's what the surveys say*. Washington, DC: author.

National Dropout Prevention Network. 1992. *Service learning: Meeting the needs of youth at risk*. Clemson, SC: author.

Newmann, F. M., and R. A. Rutter. 1983. *The effects of high school community service programs on students' social development: Final report*. Madison: University of Wisconsin Center for Educational Research.

———. 1986. A profile of national community service programs. *Educational Leadership* 43:65–71.

Noack, P., M. Hofer, and J. Youniss, eds. 1995. *Psychological responses to social change*. New York: De Gruyter.

Offer, D., E. Ostrov, and K. I. Howard. 1981. *The adolescent: A psychological self-portrait*. New York: Basic Books.

O'Neill, M. 1994. Philanthropic dimensions of mutual benefit organizations. *Nonprofit and Voluntary Sector Quarterly* 23:3–20.

Otto, L. B. 1976. Social integration and the status attainment process. *American Journal of Sociology* 81:1360–83.

People for the American Way. 1989. *Democracy's next generation: A study of youth and teachers.* Washington, DC: author.

Phinney, J. S. 1990. Ethnic identity in adolescents and adults: Review of Research. *Psychological Bulletin* 108:499–514.

Rahner, K. 1979. *Theological investigations.* Vol. 16. Translated by D. Moreland. New York: Seabury Press.

Rich, S. 1994. Number of poor Americans increases to 39.3 million. *Washington Post,* October 7, A1, A18.

Rigsby, L. C., and E. L. McDill. 1975. Value orientations of high school students. In H. R. Stubb, ed., *The sociology of education,* 53–75. Homewood, IL: Dorsey.

Rosenhan, D. L. 1970. The natural socialization of altruistic autonomy. In J. Macauley and L. Berkowitz, eds., *Altruism and helping behaviors,* 251–68. Orlando, FL: Academic Press.

Rutter, R. A., and F. M. Newmann. 1989. The potential of community service to enhance civic responsibility. *Social Education* 53:371–74.

Schlosberg, A. 1991. Seven year follow up of an adolescent volunteer program in a psychiatric hospital. *Hospital and Community Psychiatry* 42:532–33.

Sebald, H. 1986. Adolescents' shifting orientation toward parents and peers: A curvilinear trend over recent decades. *Journal of Marriage and the Family* 48:5–13.

Siegel, L. J., and J. J. Senna. 1994. *Juvenile delinquency: Theory, practice, and law.* New York: West Publishing.

Spencer, M. B., and S. M. Dornbusch. 1990. Challenges in studying minority youth. In S. S. Feldman and G. R. Elliot, eds., *At the threshold: The developing adolescent,* 123–46. Cambridge: Harvard University Press.

Stein, M. I. 1966. *Volunteers for peace: The first group of Peace Corps volunteers in a rural community in Columbia, South America.* New York: Wiley.

Steinberg, L., J. Elmen, and N. Mounts. 1989. Authoritative parenting, psychosocial maturity, and academic success among adolescents. *Child Development* 60:1424–36.

Teilhard de Chardin, P. [1955] 1975. *The phenomenon of man.* Translated by B. Wall. New York: Harper and Row.

Tesson, G., and J. Youniss. 1995. Micro-sociology and psychological development: A sociological interpretation of Piaget's theory. In M. Ambert, ed., *Sociological Studies of Children,* 7:101–26. Greenwich, CT: JAI Press.

Toren, C. 1993. Making history: The significance of childhood cognition for a comparative anthropology of mind. *Man* 28:461–78.

Townsend, K. K. 1992. The most important lesson our schools don't teach. *St. Petersburg Times,* December 27, 1D.

Tropman, J. E. 1995. *The Catholic ethic in American society: An exploration of values.* San Francisco: Jossey-Bass.

U.S. Department of Commerce. 1994. *Statistical abstract of the United States.* Washington, DC: author.

U.S. Senate. Labor and Human Resources Committee. 1990. *Senate report for National and Community Service Act of 1990.* Washington, DC: author.

Verba, S., and N. H. Nie. 1972. *Participation in America: Political democracy and social equality.* New York: Harper and Row.

Verba, S., K. L. Schlozman, and H. E. Brady. 1995. *Voice and equality: Civic volunteerism in American politics.* Cambridge, MA: Harvard University Press.

Walker, L. J., B. de Vries, and S. D. Trevethan. 1987. Moral stages and moral orientations in real-life and hypothetical dilemmas. *Child Development* 58:842–58.

Wertsch, J. 1985. *Vygotsky and the social formation of mind.* Cambridge, MA: Harvard University Press.

West, C. 1993. *Race matters.* Boston: Beacon.

Wilson, W. J. 1987. *The truly disadvantaged: The inner city, the underclass, and public policy.* Chicago: University of Chicago Press.

Wofford, H. 1995. Confirmation of Harris Wofford as CEO of the National Corporation for National and Community Service. In *Hearings of the U.S. Senate Labor and Human Resources Committee.* September 7.

Wuthnow, R. 1991. *Acts of compassion: Caring for others and helping ourselves.* Princeton, NJ: Princeton University Press.

Yardley, J. 1986. How King changed our lives. *Washington Post,* January 20, C2.

Yates, M., and J. Youniss. 1996a. Community service and political-moral identity in adolescents. *Journal of Research on Adolescence* 6:271–84.

———. 1996b. A developmental perspective on community service. *Social Development* 5:85–111.

Youniss, J. 1980. *Parents and peers in social development.* Chicago: University of Chicago Press.

———. 1993. Integrating culture and religion into developmental psychology. *Family Perspective* 26:171–88.

Youniss, J., and W. Damon. 1992. Social construction in Piaget's theory. In H. Beilin and P. P. Pufall, eds., *Piaget's theory: Prospects and possibilities,* 267–86. Hillsdale, NJ: Erlbaum.

Youniss, J., and J. Smollar. 1985. *Adolescent relations with mothers, fathers, and friends.* Chicago: University of Chicago Press.

Youniss, J., and M. Yates. 1996. Adolescents' public discussions and collective identity. Paper presented at symposium, "Verbal and nonverbal facets of communication: Social interaction, cultural practices, and development," Clark University, Worcester, April.

Youniss, J., M. Yates, and Y. Su. In press. Social integration into peer and adult society: Community service and marijuana use in high school seniors. *Journal of Adolescent Research.*

INDEX

Agency, 70ff.: component of identity, 25; development of, 78–80, 94–95, 131–32

Alliance for Service Learning in Education Reform: 135

Alumni (of St. Francis) study: 118ff.; continuity through life, 129–30; description of study, 118–22; long-term effects of service, 123–28; recall of Social Justice course, 123–24; volunteer history, 120–21

Black identity: and American identity, 109–11; consciousness of, 99–100; family histories, 111–12; generational linkages, 112–13, 149–50; Nation of Islam, 107–9, 169–70; negative images, 100–102; public figures as role models, 104–7; White teachers, 103–4, 106; universal humanity, 166–70

Blasi, A.: 1, 84, 164

Boyte, H.: 17, 69, 81, 82, 172

Bryk, A.: viii, 170ff.

Catholic ethic: viii, 96, 155

Catholic schooling: 38–39, 42–43, 140–42, 170–71

Chavez, C.: 40, 150, 155

Civic identity: 81–82; in alumni, 122

Civil rights movement: 32–36

Colby, A.: 20, 26, 157, 165

Coleman, J. S.: 9, 16, 170

Coles, R.: 172

Collins, R.: 26–27, 80

Commission and National and Community Service: 138–39

Community service: adult models, 144–47; class, 148; developmental opportunities, 3, 25, 136; in contemporary youth, 5–8; family patterns, 117, 120–21; gender, 148–49; peers, 117, 120–21; in public schools, 11, 141–42; policy recommendations, 136ff.; race, 148

Conrad, D.: 3, 8, 11, 37, 143

Contemporary youth: age segregation, 9, 15–16; characterizations, 3–9; political-moral awareness, 11–13

Corporation for National and Community Service: 135, 136, 143, 144, 147

Corsaro, W.: 26–27, 161

Cross, W.: 99, 100, 168

Damon, W.: 20, 26, 157, 165

Day, Dorothy, 40, 155

Developmental opportunities: 3, 25, 136

Discovery of the Other: 87, 123, 124

Dropping out of school: 55, 170–71

Drugs: and homelessness, 55, 85, 87; legalization, 77–78, 110

Eder, D.: 26–27, 161

Emotional engagement in service: 59–60

Erikson, E. H.: 17–18, 20, 21ff.; role of ideology, 23–24; social interpretation, 21; theory of identity development, 21ff.

Farrakhan, L.: 107–9, 169

183